THE
PRIESTLY
BLESSING

"'Then he led them (out) as far as Bethany, raised his hands, and blessed them. As he blessed them he parted from them and was taken up to heaven' (Lk 24:50–51). The first disciples recalled Jesus' Ascension culminating in his blessing them. The Church has continued that tradition of bestowing blessings upon people, things, and events. Stephen J. Rossetti has prepared a truly helpful text that traces the practice as an important part of the Church's ongoing ministry in Jesus' name. All those who have the privilege of bestowing a blessing will find the book both informative and wonderfully inspiring."

Most Rev. Wilton D. Gregory
Archbishop of Atlanta

"Stephen J. Rossetti has both written and bestowed a blessing to clergy everywhere. He has provided the biblical rationale, the pastoral preparation, and a passionate charge for clergy to be blessing their flocks at every occasion. From one who prepares permanent deacons for ordination, this is an excellent text for deacon candidates in their formative years. For those who ask for a blessing, and for those who have the (rediscovered) joy of giving a blessing, this is a wonderful book that will give grace to many."

Deacon Rick Bauer
Academic dean and instructor of sacred scripture
Permanent Diaconate Formation Program
Diocese of Colorado Springs

"In *The Priestly Blessing*, Msgr. Stephen Rossetti successfully calls upon the long tradition of the Church in her understanding of the meaning and pastoral nature of priestly blessings. While acknowledging the unique power of a blessing vested in the ordained priesthood, he also sets forth the conditions under which the laity and deacons can give blessings. Rossetti recoups the beauty and understanding of blessings as a sign of spiritual richness in the life of the Church."

Msgr. Peter J. Vaghi
Pastor of Church of the Little Flower
Bethesda, Maryland

"Stephen J. Rossetti offers an engaging invitation to rediscover the value of the ample use of blessings by clergy and also explores appropriate use of blessings by the laity. From its biblical roots to the present, a blessing connects us with the Giver of all blessings in a spirit of gratitude and petition."

Most Rev. Timothy P. Broglio
Archbishop for the Military Services, USA

"Msgr. Stephen Rossetti has written a reflection that is most encouraging and helpful for parish priests. We can easily forget the beautiful gifts that God gave us at our ordination for the benefit of his people and our own sanctification. Here is a book that reminds us of the beauty and efficacy of the priestly blessing, and blessings in general. It is a wonderful combination of what is theological and pastoral, educating and edifying. It is a gift to the Church."

Msgr. Charles Pope
Pastor of Holy Comforter-St. Cyprian Roman Catholic Church
Washington, DC

"Stephen J. Rossetti has done us a favor in redirecting our attention to the sublime gift of sacramental blessings. Every Catholic experiences this gift, but few of us have taken the time to consider it fully. This book lays out the scriptural foundations for blessings. It also gives us insight into the ecclesial dimensions and liturgical renewal that took place not so long ago. May this book lead us not only to rediscover the gift but also to a renewal of the ministry and the sanctification of God's people."

Rev. Keith Kenney
Pastor of St. Margaret Mary Catholic Church
Bullhead City, Arizona

THE
PRIESTLY
BLESSING

REDISCOVERING THE GIFT

STEPHEN J. ROSSETTI

AVE MARIA PRESS AVE Notre Dame, Indiana

Nihil Obstat: Rev. Christopher R. Seibt

Imprimatur: Most Rev. Robert J. Cunningham
Bishop of the Diocese of Syracuse
Given at Syracuse on February 28, 2018

Founded in 1865, Ave Maria Press is a ministry of the United States Province of Holy Cross.

www.avemariapress.com

Paperback: ISBN-13 978-1-59471-847-2

E-book: ISBN-13 978-1-59471-848-9

Cover image © Cinoby/iStock/Getty Images Plus.

Cover and text design by Samantha Watson.

Printed and bound in the United States of America.

Library of Congress Cataloging-in-Publication Data is available.

The Lord said to Moses:
Speak to Aaron and his sons and tell them:
This is how you shall bless the Israelites. Say to them:
The Lord bless you and keep you!
The Lord let his face shine upon you,
and be gracious to you!
The Lord look upon you kindly and give you peace!
So shall they invoke my name upon the Israelites,
and I will bless them.
—Numbers 6:22–27

CONTENTS

PREFACE

The subject of priestly blessings, and also those of deacons and the laity, seems to be garnering more interest in recent years. There are a number of blogs and podcasts by priests now published on blessings, and some priests have written STL theses on this subject. It is a topic that is starting to be discussed, especially in clerical circles. Priests spend quite a bit of time giving blessings of every sort, and yet it is a subject infrequently discussed in their intellectual and pastoral formation. And many of us have come to realize that there is a great lack of resources available to teach or learn about the history, theology, and ecclesial importance of blessing for the life of the Church.

Since we priests spend so much time giving blessings, it only makes sense that we ought to understand and be trained in the meaning and practice of the priestly blessing. In my own experience, and that of many priests I know, people regularly ask for blessings and are very grateful when such blessings are given. A few days ago, a priest told me that he was at a couple's house for a social gathering, and they asked him to bless their home. A few moments later, another couple approached and asked him to come and bless their new business. Blessings are a staple in the life of a priest. This is as it should be. Priests are ordained, as we recall from the current ordination rite, "for the sanctification of the Christian people."[1]

Moreover, I believe that, as secularism increasingly seeps into many parts of the world, God's blessings can help turn back the tide. Secularism seeks to divorce the world from its Creator. Blessings are one important way to open us to the sacredness of all creation and to God's transforming grace everywhere present in Christ. Blessings can remind us of and assist us in living each moment of our lives in the grace of God's loving presence.

A few days ago I was walking outside of the local cathedral, and a woman hobbled up with a bad knee. I gently inquired about her condition. She explained her troubles and asked me to pray for her. I nodded and said, "Would you like a blessing?" She enthusiastically said yes, and I laid my hands on her head and prayed. She was very pleased. She thanked me and was grateful for the personal attention. These spontaneous blessings can indeed be immediate, personal, pastoral encounters.

While such pastoral moments are multiplied countless times daily around the world, the nature and theology of these seemingly simple blessings is surprisingly complicated. As we look into the subject of blessings, it becomes increasingly apparent how complex the subject is. What also surfaces are the intellectual differences of opinion. Such differences reflect the ecclesial divides in our Church today.

One of my guiding principles in writing this book, and in my years of priesthood, has been a clear decision to stay in the Barque of Peter. I am a happy Catholic priest, and I cherish the beautiful Tradition that we have been given. First and foremost, I minister in obedience to my bishop, the Holy Father, and the teaching magisterium of the Church. Thus, I submitted this book to the process of securing an *imprimatur*, which, as you can see, the book does have. If there is anything in this book that unwittingly may not have been precise enough in transmitting our Tradition, I apologize for it and take sole responsibility for it.

Within the Church's Tradition, there is quite a bit of room for a valid debate and disagreement on many subjects, including the nature of blessings in particular and sacramentals in general. This book will not resolve such debates, nor do I intend it to do so.

While this book is written in full accord with the Church's magisterium, there is still plenty of room for faithful Catholics to disagree. This is how theology and pastoral practice have been accomplished for nearly two thousand years. The Church teaches us what issues have been resolved, and thus we adhere willingly to those with a filial piety. But within that Barque, there are issues to discuss. This book raises some of those issues.

In the midst of such discussions, it is important to be honest about where we agree and disagree. But always we ought to build bridges, not walls. In reality, there is much on which we all agree, including in the area of blessings. The essentials are known, taught, and affirmed. We ought first to emphasize these bedrock beliefs and those areas where we agree. These are bridges. But we can also disagree on other issues; and in the area of blessings, there is much to discuss.

There is a great need in this country, in the Church, and around the world for people to dialogue in charity with each other not only about religious matters but about practically everything. Instead of terrorism and violence—which seem to be mounting all around us, either physical or verbal—a respectful dialogue undertaken in charity is needed. I hope to contribute to this charitable dialogue, at least modestly, on this one circumscribed topic.

It is my hope that this book will be a bridge. I would like it to be a step forward in reconciling differing views. I have sought to make explicit some of the differences. Obviously, I have my own preferences, which no doubt come out in the course of this book. These arise from my own study, pastoral experience, and dialogue with friends and colleagues. But I pray that we will all listen to different perspectives with an open heart and perhaps expand our vision a bit.

This book is certainly not the final word on the subject of blessings. I welcome hearing from those who have a different perspective. We are brothers and sisters in the Lord. This book is meant only to be a little beginning.

ACKNOWLEDGMENTS

I am so very grateful to the many scholars, theologians, and pastors who reviewed this book and made important recommendations. I take responsibility for what is contained in this text, but its writing would not have been possible without their expertise and important insights. I am especially grateful to the following people, in alphabetical order: Msgr. David Bohr; Archbishop Timothy Broglio; Fr. Luke Clark, O.P.; Archbishop Wilton Gregory; Fr. Keith Kenney; Fr. Dennis McManus; Msgr. William Millea; Msgr. Charles Pope; Fr. Ryan Ruiz; Fr. Christopher Seibt; Fr. George Stuart; Msgr. Peter Vaghi; Dcn. Rhett Williams; and Fr. Michael Witczak.

ABBREVIATIONS

CCC   *Catechism of the Catholic Church*
LG   *Lumen Gentium*
SC   *Sacrosanctum Concilium*
ST   *Summa Theologica*

1.

THE GIFT
OF BLESSINGS

Everyone in the crowd sought to touch him because power
came forth from him and healed them all.
—Luke 6:19

Not long ago, I was walking through the airport, and a woman behind
one of the kiosks across the terminal shouted, "Father, pray for me!" So I
walked over to her and asked, "May I lay my hands on your head?" She
nodded. I placed my hands on her head and prayed. Then, with the Sign
of the Cross, I pronounced the words of blessing: "May almighty God bless
you, the Father, and the Son, and the Holy Spirit." This woman was not
afraid to expose her desire for a priestly blessing in front of scores of people
rushing by to catch their airplanes. Obviously she valued the blessing and
felt the need of such a blessing in that particular moment of her life. If
she was not embarrassed to ask in public, I should not be embarrassed to
bless her in front of a crowd. I was happy to do so.

Also not long ago, I attended an exorcism. At one point, the exorcist—who ministers only after receiving faculties from his diocesan bishop—laid his hands on the head of the possessed person in blessing, and the
individual started to writhe in agony. Out of her mouth came the words,
"It's burning!" The priest then sprinkled the person with holy water, and
she screamed. He later explained that the screaming came because of the

demons, who suffered a tremendous agony as they came in contact with holy water.

The exorcist further explained that, as a priest, his hands were anointed by the bishop and so themselves are a kind of sacramental. The demons suffered greatly when blessed by a priest's hands. In Luke 4:40–41, we see Jesus healing and exorcizing through the laying on of his hands: "He laid his hands on each of them and cured them. And demons also came out from many." As early as the third century, Origen referred to the imposition of hands by exorcists to cast out evil spirits as well as "many prayers . . . many fasts."[1] There is even an earlier reference to the imposition of hands to cast out an evil spirit in the Qumran *Genesis Apocryphon*, one of the Dead Sea Scrolls. Abram exorcizes an "evil spirit" from the pharaoh by laying his hands on him.[2]

Steven LaChance reviewed the famous exorcism case that inspired the terrifying 1973 movie *The Exorcist*. In his book *Confrontation with Evil*, he described his own experience of being prayed over by a priest when he was personally oppressed by demonic forces:

> Catholicism is not my faith, and in fact, at the time I was struggling with my faith in general. So one could imagine how shocked I was by the physical reaction my body was having to Catholic blessings, as the father began to pray. I could not breathe, almost like a severe asthma attack. I was sweating profusely even though it was a cool autumn day. I was on the brink of passing out, breathing quick shallow breaths, and it felt as if I had an elephant sitting on my chest. But through all this chaos, I could still hear the priest praying, fighting for my soul. Just when I thought I could not stand it anymore and I wanted to give up, I saw three bright white flashes, which made an audible sound in my ears. As each flash ascended forth, air found its way back into my lungs, and I felt this overwhelming sense of peace and calm. It was a feeling of euphoria and I wanted it to remain with me forever.[3]

In this passage, the author described the power of what he called "Catholic blessings" as the priest was "fighting for my soul." And then, with the demonic presence apparently gone, he experienced an "overwhelming sense of peace" and a kind of euphoria that sounds almost ecstatic.[4]

We priests spend quite a bit of our time laying hands on people's heads in prayer and blessing. More than a few times every week we move our hands in the air, making the Sign of the Cross, and give a blessing. We do so at the end of every Mass, saying the words of absolution in the confessional, and in a variety of liturgical and nonliturgical settings. For us, it is part of the daily tasks of a priest.

We may not attach much significance to it. When people request such a blessing from us, perhaps because of an illness or maybe to bless their rosaries or crucifixes, the benign thought may go through our minds, "Why not, it can't hurt," or perhaps, "It's a good, pious thing to do." We have an idea that it is indeed a good thing, but the significance of the act is little known and, I think, underappreciated.

What if Steven LaChance's experience of a priestly prayer and "blessing" in the Rite of Exorcism is actually more accurate than what our mundane thinking might ascribe to it? What if the priestly blessing carries a powerful divine grace that makes demons flee and imparts divine peace and calm? If it does, then we ought to rethink the way we minister as priests. If so, then it ought to reenergize our daily actions when we bless and pray over the people and things around us. It ought to help us rediscover the power of the ordained priesthood and the dynamic presence of Christ in his Church.

Acknowledging the divine grace offered in the priestly blessing is a recognition of the dynamic presence of Christ in his Church and the authority given to its ministers.

There is little written on this subject of priestly blessings. During my years as a seminarian, I do not recall it ever being mentioned. In fact, during my priestly formation more than thirty-five years ago, instructors seemed concerned with not promoting clericalism and downplayed any special grace attached to the priesthood.

Indeed, clericalism is a horrible scourge on the priesthood and the People of God. If our instructors were quick to eschew any tints of clericalism, it is because they were reacting to obvious forms of clericalism that people experienced in the past. Pope Francis, in particular, rightly continues to excoriate any hint of it. In a 2016 morning Mass homily addressing the Council of Cardinal Advisers he said, "The spirit of clericalism is an evil that is present in the Church today."[5]

And yet, people continue to ask priests to bless them. The history of blessings suggests that blessings have arisen from the needs and piety of the People of God, and that they were not typically inventions of the hierarchy. Blessings are concrete ways that people have incorporated the sacred into their daily lives. They are an expression of the people's belief that God can and does act in their daily lives and through the stuff of this earth. If the Church's rituals and practice value blessings, it is because the Church takes seriously the people's desires and their needs.

Blessings also express the fears and anxieties of the people.[6] During the Gulf War, a soldier clad in battle fatigues was on his way to a combat zone. He spied me at the airport and walked over. He was obviously a bit nervous and, in a crowded airport terminal, asked me for a blessing. I laid my hands on his head and blessed him, to the curious looks of bystanders. It was a public act of faith on his part and on mine.

Many of the faithful earnestly desire the blessing of a priest, especially in moments of need. They instinctively know that the priesthood carries a unique grace from God. They may not come to church, but the spark of faith is still alive in them. And in moments of need, they turn to God for help, as they should. When they see someone ordained by the Church to bring God's grace to them, they instinctively reach out to him.[7]

Of course, the importance of a blessing can be exaggerated. In some Catholic parishes, those who are not Catholic, or Catholics not properly disposed to receive Communion, are invited to come up for a blessing at Communion time.[8] But one Catholic woman, after properly receiving Eucharist at the Mass, said to me that she was a bit envious of those who received the priestly blessing. It was as if those who received a blessing received more. At such moments we might be reminded that sacramentals, of which the priestly blessing is one, are oriented toward the sacraments and not vice versa.

Nevertheless, there are signs that some people, including priests, are losing a sense of the importance of the priest's blessing. When we priests and laity downplay the power of the priestly blessing, we are ultimately losing a sense of the importance of the Church. The priest is appointed and ordained to bless in the name of the Church. The priestly blessing is a concrete instance of the Church herself blessing. When reverence for the grace of the priesthood wanes, reverence for the Church follows quickly behind it.

The subject of priestly blessings is complicated and multivalent. As we shall see, the word *blessing* refers to many things. It can refer to a consecration of something for liturgical use, such as a chalice. In this case, we say the chalice has been blessed or consecrated. Blessings are also an integral part of sacramental graces, such as the nuptial blessing in a marriage or the final blessing typically found at the end of rites of sacraments. We can speak about blessings as a separate liturgical event, as envisioned in the revised *Book of Blessings* promulgated for use in the United States in 1989. These blessings include scriptural readings, responsorials, invocations, and prayers of blessing. Blessings can also be more informal, spontaneous pastoral acts, such as when someone walks up and asks for a personal blessing or the blessing of a religious object. Then the priest will typically make the Sign of the Cross and say a spontaneous prayer of blessing.

Exorcists will sometimes tell the possessed person that they are going to give the person a "blessing," thus using the Church's Rite of Exorcism, itself a sacramental, to expel evil spirits in accord with its long tradition stemming directly from the ministry of Jesus. The greatest blessing is when the priest "blesses" God over the bread and wine at the Mass, thus transforming them into the Body and Blood of Christ. All these are called "blessings," and while they arise from different contexts and carry different meanings, they are inseparably linked in the one God who is the source of each and every blessing. It is God's saving grace in Jesus that redeems all of creation and is active in each of these kinds of graced acts that we call blessings.

It might be important for us who bless, and for those who ask for blessings, to step back and look at this history, theology, and practice of blessings. It might be important for us to understand more fully what it is that we are doing. Such knowledge will help us to appreciate more fully the gift that God has given to us, the authority entrusted to the Church, and the saving power of Jesus Christ.

In order to better understand priestly blessings, we begin by looking to the sacred scriptures and then to Church history and centuries of pastoral practice. We will investigate what the saints and the Doctors of the Church have told us. And, of course, we will rely on the teaching of the Catholic Church to guide us at every step.

As we weave our way through the Old Testament, the New Testament, Church history, and the Church's official teaching on blessings, we will begin to discover the rich tradition that we have inherited. It will help us to understand why we bless the way we do, and we will begin to discover the ancient roots of our pastoral practice. As I engaged in research for this text, I found myself becoming excited about giving blessings. I began to realize what a wonderful grace our generous God offers to his people through this Church sacramental. I began to cherish even more the priesthood of Jesus Christ. I hope this book does the same for you.

2.

BLESSINGS IN THE OLD TESTAMENT

I will bless the LORD at all times;
  his praise shall be always in my mouth.
                                    —Psalm 34:2

The notion of blessings is not new. It is not something that began in the Middle Ages. In fact, it is older than even the Old Testament. Primitive cultures incorporated ideas of blessings. But what the Old Testament began, and the New Testament continued to develop, was a rejection of any *magical* notions of blessings.[1] In the Judeo-Christian tradition, all blessings come from God. And beginning with the New Testament, they are now mediated through the Son, Jesus Christ.[2]

God is the source of all blessings; no magical understandings are proper to Judeo-Christianity.

Be Fertile and Multiply

The very first biblical blessing in general, and the first blessing of animals in particular, occurs in Genesis 1:22. God blessed the first animals he created. "God blessed them, saying: 'Be fertile, multiply, and fill the water of the seas; and let the birds multiply on the earth.'" Then God blessed the first male and female he created. "God blessed them and God said to them: 'Be fertile and multiply; fill the earth and subdue it'" (Gn 1:28). God's imparting a blessing both to humans and to animals was thought to be important because procreative power was seen as coming only from God. God was recognized as the Author of all life, and thus it was his power that allowed them to bring forth life.[3]

It is also appropriate that the first blessing came from God himself. It reminds us that all blessings come from God, including, of course, the priestly blessing. Such a reminder should be a healthy curb against any manifestations of clericalism: God is the source of all life and all blessings. This will be an important theme running throughout this book.

The Hebrew root for blessing is *bārak* the word for blessing is *berakah*. As the *Sacramentum Verbi* points out, the word has a broader meaning than the English word.[4] Historian Derek Rivard wrote, "The act of blessing, *barakh*, was understood as the imparting of vital power to another person, thus giving another a part of the blessing of one's soul originally bestowed by God."[5] That power, ultimately derived from God as the source, can manifest itself in many salutary ways.

A blessing can have a variety of meanings that are translated into English using different words, depending upon the context. For example, *bārak* can be linked to fertility, as it is here in Genesis. God's blessing brings prosperity in the form of offspring. Hebrews who had no children felt most unfortunate and perhaps even cursed. Elizabeth, Mary's cousin, spoke of her childlessness as a "disgrace before others" (Lk 1:25), as did Rachel before her (see Gn 30:23). Recognizing the true blessing of having children might be an especially important grace for our day!

The blessing of children is perhaps one of the most fundamental blessings in this life, finding its origin in God and the foundation of creation. Looking at the beaming faces of new parents reminds me of this grace. We priests ought to be especially supportive of new parents and the challenges of parenthood. We also should be most solicitous in those sad cases where couples are willing but not able to conceive. Continuing life and passing on the faith are humankind's most sacred responsibilities.

BLESS THE LORD

Interestingly, a blessing in Old Testament times could also be in reference to people "blessing" God. In the same book, Genesis, we read, "Then I knelt and bowed down to the LORD, blessing the LORD, the God of my master Abraham, who had led me on the right road" (Gn 24:48). In this context, "blessing" refers to praising God. Some have suggested that the word *bārak* is related to the Hebrew word *berek*, meaning "knee." Hence to "bless" God implies an act of worship on one's knees.

An important use of the word "bless" refers to blessing God. In the Jewish *berakah*, we praise and "bless" God for his overwhelming generosity to us, and we thank him.

For failing to worship the god of King Nebuchadnezzar, Shadrach, Meshach, and Abednego were thrown into the white-hot furnace. God miraculously saved them; and, in unison, they blessed God with an ecstatic song of praise: "Blessed are you, O Lord, the God of our ancestors, praise-worthy and exalted above all forever" (Dn 3:52). The three young men then went on to exhort all of creation to bless the Lord, perhaps reminding us of St. Francis's Canticle of the Sun. They sang, "Sun and moon, bless the Lord. . . . Stars of heaven, bless the Lord. . . . Fire and heat, bless the Lord. . . . Cold and chill, bless the Lord" (Dn 3:62, 63, 66, 67). All of creation was invited to join in their exultant song of praise.

Similarly, there are many types of psalms, but one type is called the psalm of blessing. In these psalms, the author sings the praise of God. Again, to praise God and to bless God are synonymous. For example, in Psalm 34: "I will bless the LORD at all times; his praise shall be always in my mouth" (v. 2). Also in Psalm 104, we are invited in the first verse to "bless the LORD, my soul! LORD my God, you are great indeed!" Psalm 104 goes on to praise God as Creator of the universe. He is the one who "spread out the heavens like a tent" (v. 2) and "fixed the earth on its foundation" (v. 5). He "made springs flow in wadies" (v. 10), and he "made the moon to mark the seasons" (v. 19). In his creation, we see the glory of God manifest, and we pray, "May the glory of the LORD endure forever" (v. 31).

In Psalm 103 we read, "Bless the LORD, my soul; all my being, bless his holy name! Bless the LORD, my soul; and do not forget all his gifts" (vv. 1–2). The psalmist (and we too!) goes on to enumerate the reasons for our praise of God. God is praised because of his many blessings or gifts that he gives to us; he is praised for his goodness. He is praised because he is "merciful" (v. 8) and "has compassion on his children" (v. 13). Also, he "pardons" and "heals" (v. 3). Most importantly, he "redeems your life from the pit" (v. 4)—that is, he saves or delivers you from danger and destruction. This is a foreshadowing of the ultimate salvation in which God's deliverance or salvation of the human race will be definitive and eternal. This is a wonderful litany of the reasons why we praise (bless) the Lord.

Most importantly, however, we praise God for just being who he is. God is infinite love, beauty, and truth. When we gaze upon the Lord, we are completely overwhelmed with such goodness, and praise spontaneously leaps up from our hearts. Our mouths burst forth God's praise: "Bless the Lord!" We need no other reason to praise God than this.

BLESS THE GRAIN AND THE WINE AND THE OIL

As noted previously, Genesis speaks of God's primordial blessing of human beings and animals. In the Old Testament, blessings apply not only to animals and people but also to God's creation. In Deuteronomy we read: "He [God] will love and bless and multiply you; he will bless the fruit of your womb and the produce of your soil, your grain and wine and oil, the young of your herds and the offspring of your flocks" (7:13). And again, in Exodus: "You shall serve the LORD, your God; then he will bless your food and drink" (23:25).

God blessed all of creation. God called it to be fruitful and multiply.

The blessings of the fruits of the field were linked to the righteousness of the people to whom they belonged. God's creation itself properly receives God's blessings, but most especially when linked to the human person, who is called to have dominion over the earth (see Gn 1:28). "His blessing rests upon all of creation but preeminently upon human beings."[6] These notions will be especially important in understanding the post–Vatican II revised *Book of Blessings*. Later in this book, when we look at these newer blessings, we will see that creation is thought to be blessed through its service to God's people and through its proper use.

Unlike animals and creation, the human person can choose. Thus, God's blessings for people are linked to choosing him—that is, "loving the LORD, your God, obeying his voice, and holding fast to him" (Dt 30:20). The choice is stark: "I have set before you life and death, the blessing and the curse" (Dt 30:19).[7] The reward for choosing God—that is, choosing life—will be a "long life for you to live on the land which the LORD swore to your ancestors" (Dt 30:20).

God's blessing for his people who love and follow him was thought to be a long life on this earth in the promised land. This is the land that is filled with God's material blessings, "flowing with milk and honey" (see, for example, Ex 3:8, 3:17; Lv 20:24; Nm 13:27, 14:8; Dt 11:9, 26:9, 31:20). Thus, God blessed the righteous and blessed their lives with longevity and abundance.

God especially blessed men and women and gave them dominion over the earth. God's blessings would descend on those who heard his voice and held fast to him.

Presumably = maybe

GIVEN AUTHORITY TO BLESS

In Old Testament times, some individuals were given authority to bless by virtue of their position, presumably given by God. For example, the patriarchs had the authority to impart a blessing.[8] Noah blessed his son Shem (see Gn 9:26). Jacob blessed his grandsons: "Bring them to me . . . that I may bless them" (Gn 48:9). Perhaps reminding us of Jesus' embracing and kissing of children, Jacob gathered the two children, and then "he kissed and embraced them" (Gn 48:10).

Moses blessed the people in God's name as well. As the book of Exodus tells us, "When Moses saw that all the work was done just as the LORD had commanded, he blessed them" (39:43). Again, "Moses and Aaron went into the tent of meeting. On coming out they blessed the people" (Lv 9:23). So too did Moses's successor Joshua bless people: "Joshua blessed Caleb, son of Jephunneh, and gave him Hebron as his heritage" (Jos 14:13).

Similarly, kings blessed people. When the ark of the Lord was brought in, David offered sacrifices, and "he blessed the people in the name of the LORD of hosts" (2 Sm 6:18). So rulers over the people could give blessings, presumably because their authority came from God. Pagan cultures often believed in a type of divine authority residing in their leaders, some even positing that they were deities themselves. Similarly, God commanded Samuel to anoint Saul as "ruler of my people Israel" because "this is the man I told you about; he shall govern my people" (1 Sm 9:16–17). Saul's authority to rule was, therefore, thought to come directly from God.

In Europe, for hundreds of years, monarchs claimed some divine authority to rule. Some even claimed they were above any human law and could only be judged by God. Today, this meshing of divine authority and human rule has waned, and secular authorities would typically not presume to offer a blessing from God or claim to govern based upon divine authority.

In Old Testament times, priests had a special authority given by God to bless the people. In Deuteronomy we read, "The priests, the descendants of Levi, shall come forward, for the LORD, your God, has chosen them to minister to him and to bless in the name of the LORD" (21:5). Here we see a clear reference to priests being consecrated to the Lord and given a special office of blessing the people. This is also found in Deuteronomy

10:8: "The LORD set apart the tribe of Levi . . . to stand before the LORD to minister to him, and to bless in his name, as they have done to this day."

In Old Testament times, priests were set apart or consecrated. They were empowered to give blessings in God's name.

This special authority of priests is echoed in 1 Chronicles: "Aaron was set apart to be consecrated as most holy, he and his sons forever, to offer sacrifice before the LORD, to minister to him, and to bless in his name forever" (23:13). In this case, an integral part of their office is to "bless in his name." Thus, priests are tasked with the twofold mission of praising God and blessing his people.

Today, no one would consider that the elected president of a country could give a blessing reputed to be a grace from God. He or she would be thought to be usurping divine authority, and such an act would be viewed as a dangerous reversion to ancient theocratic rule. This separation of church and state, and thus the separation of divine and human power, is one of the benefits of modern secularity. Today, it remains the prerogative and the function of religious authority, consecrated by God, to bless.

A PARENT'S BLESSING

Parents have the right and obligation to bless their children. In Sirach we read, "A father's blessing gives a person firm roots" (3:9). In this book, we read of the children's obligations toward their parents. Children should bring "honor" to their mothers (3:6) and should "honor" their fathers (3:8). If children "in word and deed honor" their fathers, then "all blessings may come to" them (3:8). In turn, the father blesses his children. On the contrary, children who "neglect their father" and "provoke their mother" are "accursed" (3:16).

The Catholic Church recognizes the authority of parents to bless their children. The revised post–Vatican II *Book of Blessings* includes an Order for the Blessing of Sons and Daughters. In this blessing, after the reading of sacred scripture and the intercessions, the parents trace the Sign of the Cross on the foreheads of their children and recite the prayer of blessing. In the prayer, the parents invoke God's blessing upon their children.[9]

It is noted in the revised *Book of Blessings* that parents may want to bless their children on any number of pastoral occasions, such as at the beginning of the school year or during celebrations for the children.[10] Certainly a birthday could be an occasion for such a blessing.

If the child is sick, the parents may use the "Blessing of the Sick (Children)" found later in the book.[11] They pray that God might "raise up these children from their sickness," and they trace the Sign of the Cross on their foreheads.[12] One could easily imagine a parent blessing his or her children in bed at night before they sleep, particularly if their sleep is troublesome or difficult. Priests may want to instruct parents at baptisms about parents' authority to bless their children and also encourage them to do so on appropriate occasions.

The priestly blessing and the blessing of parents both find their source in God, who is the source of all blessings. Both priestly blessings and parental blessings offer a grace to the child. Despite the well-recognized authority of parents, the notes preceding the Order for the Blessing of Sons and Daughters in the revised *Book of Blessings* stipulate: "When a priest or deacon is present, the ministry of blessing more fittingly belongs to him."[13] When the priest blesses, in a unique way he stands in the person of Christ, the head of the Church: *in persona Christi capitis* (*CCC* 1548).

However, this is not to denigrate the blessing of a parent. In fact, the baptismal priesthood and the ordained priesthood are different in essence, not degree, and thus the blessings they give must likewise be different (*LG* 10; *CCC* 1592). I would suggest that the blessing that a parent gives is not completely replaceable by the priestly blessing. We priests should encourage parents to bless their children.

Modern psychology has helped us to be acutely aware that the love and blessing of a parent is irreplaceable. It is more difficult for someone who has not felt the love of a parent to understand and accept the love of God. A parent's love and blessing opens up the child in a unique and irreplaceable way to God's saving love. As parents bless their children with their love, an important grace from God, our loving Father, is given.

The Church recognizes the authority of parents to bless their children. Parents' love and blessing of their children is irreplaceable. A good pastoral initiative would be to promote a regular use by parents of the ritual blessing of their children.

One can imagine situations in which a parent's blessing would be most pastorally appropriate and perhaps preferred. As noted previously, celebrating the anniversary of the child's birth would be a wonderful setting for the parents to invoke God's blessing on their children. Or when the parents see their child off to college, this too could be a poignant moment for the parents' blessing. It would be a good pastoral initiative to promote a regular use of this Catholic ritual blessing of parents over their children.

ISAAC BLESSING HIS SON JACOB

The paternal authority to bless one's children is seen in the well-known story of Isaac being deceived and blessing Jacob instead of Esau. Isaac was old and blind. On his deathbed, it was his intention to give his eldest son, Esau, his deathbed blessing, presumably to indicate his right of inheritance (Gn 27:29): "May peoples serve you, and nations bow down to you; Be master of your brothers." Moreover, it was thought that a deathbed blessing had a special power. Isaac told his son he wanted to give him his special blessing before he died (see Gn 27:4).

Jacob, at the instigation of his mother, deceived his father, and so Isaac mistakenly gave his blessing to the younger son, Jacob, rather than the eldest, Esau. When the ruse was discovered, Esau was distraught and sobbed, begging his father for his own blessing, "Father, bless me too!" (Gn 27:34). But Isaac responded that Jacob had "carried off your blessing" (Gn 27:35), and he denied Esau's request. In fact, Isaac said, "I blessed him. Now he is blessed!" (Gn 27:33).

It might seem odd to our modern ears that Isaac believed he could not revoke his blessing from Jacob, despite it being obtained under false pretenses. But it was believed that once a blessing was given, something concrete was transmitted and it could not be revoked. The Hebrew word *dabar* can mean both "word" and "act." They recognized that words had power to them that, once spoken, had a real effect.

Today, in our increasingly desacralized culture, one might say, "They are only words." But the ancient Old Testament culture had a sense of the real power of the word. To illustrate, when we hurt someone with our words, we might then say, "I didn't mean it." But the damage is already done. The pain has already been inflicted. We can apologize after, but apologies do not completely take away the wound.

This is one of the reasons why gossip, slander, and malicious speech are sinful. We might think, "What difference does it make? These words don't really hurt anyone." But, in fact, they do. In some way, perhaps unseen, the object of the bad speech is likely harmed; and the purveyor of the words has, by uttering the slander, certainly been harmed.

It is no accident that Jesus himself is called the "Word." He is the ultimate Word of the Father, which, when spoken by God, brings life to all of creation and re-creates it in the redemption. It is this very Word that carries the complete power of the divine.

It might remind us of the power of the sacraments and, in a subordinate way, the power of sacramentals. In sacraments, the words, spoken by someone given the power to do so and over the proper matter, bring about a direct, spiritual effect. In sacramentals, as we shall see later in this text, the graced effects are offered through the intercession of the Church. If priests and deacons lose a sense of this sacramentality and the true presence of God's grace acting through them in the world, they will certainly feel their ministry becoming crippled, if not meaningless. The cleric who enters openly and willingly into this reality is one who will certainly feel greatly needed and himself empowered by this ministry.

THE REALITY OF CURSES

It is interesting that Isaac ended his blessing of Jacob by saying, "Cursed be those who curse you, and blessed be those who bless you" (Gn 27:29). Many of us do not believe curses carry much weight and believe they are probably just a lot of empty blustering. But this was not the thought in ancient times, including among the Semitic peoples.[14] For example, we find curses in the book of Genesis. Noah cursed Canaan because of the actions of Canaan's father, Ham, one of Noah's sons: "Cursed be Canaan! The lowest of slaves shall he be to his brothers" (Gn 9:25).

Just as the words of blessing carry an innate power to them, so too words used in a curse were thought to be destructive in themselves. "People in antiquity attributed a very real efficacy to the spoken word, they believed that scoffing at any given person really aroused destructive powers and could diminish his happiness."[15]

Because of the power of the word, a true prophet was especially feared. The words of false prophets were to be ignored, but the words of the prophet chosen by God had an innate power. When God's prophet blessed, the people were blessed. And when he cursed, they were cursed. The prophet, inspired and empowered by God, could pronounce a curse that would be effective.

In Numbers 22, the spiritual man and seer Balaam was sought out by the king of Moab for help. The king feared the Israelites because of their great numbers. So he asked Balaam to "curse the people for me" since "they are stronger than I am" (v. 6). The king added, "For I know that whoever you bless is blessed and whoever you curse is cursed" (v. 6).

People were thought necessarily to be cursed if they broke covenant with God. In Jeremiah we read, "Cursed be anyone who does not observe the words of this covenant" (11:3). Those who followed the Lord and kept his covenant were blessed, but those who did not were automatically cursed. Indeed, as the *Jerome Biblical Commentary* notes, "All covenantal ceremonies were concluded by blessings if the stipulations had been respected and by curses if they had not."[16] We see this in Deuteronomy: "A blessing for obeying the commandments of the LORD . . . a curse if you do not obey" (11:27–28).

The prophet Jeremiah engaged in a symbolic action that prophesized the great evil that would be visited on Jerusalem. At the Potsherd Gate, in the presence of some priests and elders, he took a clay pot and smashed it, symbolizing the destruction of the city. He pronounced this curse because "they have forsaken me [God] and profaned this place by burning incense to other gods." Moreover, they "burn their children in fire as offerings to Baal," which God found abhorrent: "something I never considered or said or commanded" (Jer 19:1–5). When Jeremiah symbolically enacted this prophecy, the ancient world believed that the words of the curse were put into motion. Jeremiah's prophecy was clear that these words were not considered magical; rather, it was the "LORD of hosts" who "will bring upon this city all the evil . . . because they have become stubborn and have not obeyed my words" (Jer 19:15).

Thus, one can understand why the people of that day tried to silence such prophets. For example, Amaziah told the prophet Amos, in the wake of his dire prophecies, to flee and "never again prophesy in Bethel" (Am 7:12–13). Amos responded with a stinging curse: "Your wife shall become a prostitute in the city, and your sons and daughters shall fall by the sword. And you yourself shall die in an unclean land" (Am 7:17). Similarly, the men of Anathoth were seeking to kill the prophet Jeremiah and command-ed him, "Do not prophesy in the name of the LORD; otherwise you shall die by our hand" (Jer 11:21). They feared the prophesies of Jeremiah, which were a "constant message of doom."[17]

However, God is all-powerful and a just judge. While human beings may be powerless to retract their curses, God can annul curses, and it is God who ultimately grants all blessings or retracts them. As noted in the book of Numbers, the prophet Balaam said, "How can I lay a curse on the one whom God has not cursed?" (Nm 23:8). The prophet has no ability to curse if it is not in accord with God's will.[18]

To believe in the power of the word is not to succumb to magic but rather to believe that human beings can be, in some manner, the instru-ments of God. This is true and most potent when the individual is partic-ularly chosen by God to impart divine blessings—and curses. The words of these individuals, God's priests and prophets, carry great power because they are acting in God's name.

BLESSING AS CONSECRATION

In Old Testament times, a blessing could also refer to a consecration, something set aside for sacred use. Some things were consecrated simply by the act of being used for a holy purpose. Soldiers who fought in holy wars were automatically consecrated to God. Priests because of their service in the Temple were also automatically consecrated.[19]

Both soldiers and priests were obliged to certain acts of purity because of their service. Soldiers were to abstain from sexual contact (segregated from women) during the time of war (see 1 Sm 21:6; 2 Sm 11:11). A priest was also required to act in accord with stricter laws of purity because "I, the LORD, make him holy" (Lv 21:15).

In Exodus 29 there is the rite for ordaining or consecrating the priests. Aaron, the high priest, is anointed with oil: "Pour it on his head, and anoint him" (v. 7). He is clothed with his sacerdotal vestments, including a breastplate, a tunic, an embroidered belt, the ephod, and a turban with a sacred diadem. His sons, also priests, are clothed with tunics, sashes, and skullcaps. "Thus shall you install Aaron and his sons" (v. 9; see also Lv 8).

The Catholic priest today is likewise "blessed" or "consecrated" or, in this case, ordained by his bishop. The ordinand lies on the floor while the Litany of the Saints is chanted. He is anointed with oil. The bishop lays his hands on the ordinand's head and prays the consecratory prayer. The priest is thus set aside for God's service.

In the case of the ordination of a priest, his consecration is a sacrament. The priest is ordained through the laying on of hands and prayers of the bishop, and he himself becomes a kind of sacramental. Some suggest his hands themselves become sacramentals, having been anointed with oil. The pious practice of the faithful kissing the hands of the priest, while somewhat embarrassing to priests, might be seen as a sign of this belief. And as I remind priests, if their hands are anointed and have become a kind of sacramental, they ought not be used for sinful purposes!

One of the common signs of blessings is for the priest to lay his hands on the person or object to be blessed, signifying the importance of the hands and touching. It suggests a kind of physical and direct transmission of God's grace. The laying on of hands can effect the passing on of the Spirit in ministry and the dedication of something to God.[20]

For example, Moses laid his hands on Joshua, which transmitted the "spirit of wisdom" and confirmed his succession to Moses's leadership: "Now Joshua, son of Nun, was filled with the spirit of wisdom, since Moses had laid his hands upon him; and so the Israelites gave him their obedience, just as the LORD had commanded Moses" (Dt 34:9).[21] Also, in the commissioning of Paul and Barnabas, "the holy Spirit said, 'Set apart for me Barnabas and Saul for the work to which I have called them.' Then, completing their fasting and prayer, they laid hands on them and sent them off" (Acts 13:2–3).[22]

Priests are consecrated or set aside for a sacred ministry by the bishop through the prayers and the laying on of hands (*CCC* 1538). A common sign in blessings is the laying on of hands, which signifies the transmission of God's grace and can also mean a dedication to God's service.

Thus the priest is ordained and set aside for a sacred ministry. It is a serious step when a priest abandons his priesthood. One would not think of returning a consecrated golden chalice to daily use at the table for meals. We would not dare take the bread consecrated at the Mass and return it for normal table use. While this should not denigrate the grace of one's daily bread, the Eucharistic bread would never be placed on the same level. What has been set aside solely for divine use should remain so.[23]

This should not incite sentiments of clericalism or spiritual pride, but it should raise up sentiments of awe and wonder at the heights of the divine graces bestowed upon the Catholic Church in general and on its priests in particular. Such graces are first and foremost given for the welfare of the People of God in service.

In addition, recognizing that one has been blessed and consecrated as a priest carries the additional duties of focusing one's mind and heart on the things of God. In the beginning of one's priesthood, such duties may, at times, feel like a burden. But as the priest becomes accustomed to "swimming" in a sea of grace, the daily dispensation of the sacraments, and a regular blessing of the world around him, God's joy slowly fills his heart and gratitude should naturally escape from his lips. As God has richly blessed him, he should increasingly bless God's creation in return.

The Aaronic Priestly Blessing

Perhaps most well known among priestly blessings, especially in the Old Testament, is the Aaronic priestly blessing in Numbers 6. This solemn blessing may still be used by priests in the dismissal at the end of Mass.

> The LORD bless you and keep you!
> The LORD let his face shine upon you,
>   and be gracious to you!
> The LORD look upon you kindly and give you peace! (Nm
>   6:24–26)[24]

In addition to the blessing itself, what is equally important in this scripture passage is the command of God to Moses that precedes it and the promise that follows it. God said to Moses, "This is how you shall bless the Israelites," and then he added, "And I will bless them" (Nm 6:23, 27).

God commands Moses to relay this blessing to Aaron and to his sons. He promises to bless the people when the priest blesses them. God told Moses emphatically, "I will bless them." If the priesthood of Aaron truly conferred God's blessing, how much more confidence should the priests who are ordained into the priesthood of Jesus Christ have in their blessings!

The intermediary role of the priest is something that can be difficult for some individuals to understand, particularly those from other faith traditions. The special role of the priest in the dispensation of salvation is strongly Catholic. Yet we see its roots here even in some of the earliest Old Testament scriptures.

Christians rightly emphasize that it is God who is the source of all grace and blessing. And as demonstrated in the next chapter on the New Testament, Jesus Christ alone is our Savior. To these divine truths, we surely and gladly must adhere. Jesus comes to us in many ways. In the economy of salvation, Jesus comes to us directly at times, without being mediated, but he also comes to us regularly through the "stuff" of the world. For example, the Word is present in all of his creation. He comes to us hidden in the matter of the sacraments. He is also hidden behind the very earthy matter of the Catholic priest in the administration of these sacraments and blessings.

When one of the faithful comes to a priest for a blessing, it is an act of faith in the Incarnation of Jesus Christ and faith in the Church he founded. When we priests respond in charity, we are affirming their faith. Our response is also our own act of faith. The priest administers rich graces in the sacraments and also, in an auxiliary way, in the sacramentals and blessings. But we priests, too, are taken up in these consecratory moments, and we too are richly blessed. Thus, our ministry is a daily blessing for us as well.

In the act of blessing, the faithful and the priests are both richly blessed.

3.

BLESSINGS IN THE NEW TESTAMENT

Then he embraced them and blessed them, placing his hands on them.

—Mark 10:16

BLESSINGS AS PRAISING GOD

The New Testament builds on the Old Testament understanding of blessings and transforms it. The word in New Testament Greek for "blessing" is *eulogia*. Like *berakah*, it can have a variety of meanings. First, it can mean the praise of God. Also, it can invoke a blessing or benefit from God. Further, it can be used when something or someone is consecrated to God.

In the first understanding of the word "blessing," the New Testament has many examples of individuals, filled with a special grace, praising or blessing God. In the infancy narratives, filled with grace and the Holy Spirit, people ecstatically bless God. For example, Zechariah was struck dumb because of his encounter with and disbelief of the angel's news. His tongue was loosed when he named his newborn son John. In his canticle, Zechariah, "filled with the holy Spirit," ecstatically proclaimed, "Blessed be the LORD, the God of Israel" (Lk 1:67–68). Similarly, Simeon held the child Jesus in his arms in the Temple and "blessed God, saying, 'Now, Master, you may let your servant go in peace'" (Lk 2:28–29).

A blessing can be many different things based upon who offers it and in what context. But it is always about our generous God, the divine plan of salvation, and how God showers his grace on all of creation.

Clearly these are all grace-filled moments, and the speaker, filled with God's joyful presence in the Spirit, praises him. It might remind one of the joy-filled praise of God in the book of Revelation, when the angels, beholding the face of God, exclaim, "Holy, holy, holy is the Lord God almighty" (Rv 4:8).

This will be our lot in heaven. Filled with the Holy Spirit and enrapt in the vision of God, we will shout with the angels, "Holy, holy, holy!" and praise the Lord. On this side of heaven, there are moments when we are especially blessed by God with his grace. We "return" the blessing by praising God. It is God alive in us who enables us to truly praise him. Indeed, the very fact that we bless God implies that we ourselves have already been blessed by God.

BLESSED ARE THE LOWLY

In the Visitation narrative, Mary's cousin Elizabeth ecstatically proclaimed Mary as uniquely blessed by God: "Most blessed are you among women, and blessed is the fruit of your womb. . . . Blessed are you who believed" (Lk 1:42, 45). In her canticle Mary exclaims, "For he has looked upon his handmaid's lowliness; behold, from now on will all ages call me blessed" (Lk 1:48).

While building on Old Testament notions of blessings, the New Testament transforms our understanding of blessings. It connects blessings with faith and with lowliness. Mary is blessed because she believed in the Lord's words to her. This will be echoed later in Luke's gospel: "Rather, blessed are those who hear the word of God and observe it" (11:28). Mary is identified from the beginning as uniquely blessed because she is a woman of faith.

She is likewise blessed because of her lowliness—that is, her humility. In her Magnificat, she exclaimed that God has "dispersed the arrogant of mind," and he has "thrown down the rulers" but "lifted up the lowly" (Lk 1:51–52).

This teaching will be explicitly codified in Jesus' Sermon on the Plain in Luke's gospel.[1] He proclaimed those "blessed" who are poor, who hunger, who weep, and who are persecuted because of the Son of Man. But he added four "woes" or, in Old Testament language, curses. Woe to those who are rich, to those who are filled, to those who laugh, and to those of whom people speak well (see Lk 6:20–26).

As in the Old Testament, those who follow God's way will be blessed, but those who do not are cursed. However, in the New Testament, Jesus' Beatitudes stand worldly values on their heads because he pronounced blessings on the lowest. Just as God blessed Mary in her lowliness, so too will God bless us in our humility and meekness. In the kingdom of God, the mighty will be cast down, and God will raise up the lowly.

Does this suggest that the priest should especially focus his ministry of blessing on the lowly, the meek, the suffering, and the disenfranchised? Pope Francis has personally focused his ministry on the poor and suffering, and his example suggests that we do the same. Jesus pronounces that the poor and suffering are especially blessed.

Our ministry ought to have a special focus on the poor and suffering, whom Jesus said are blessed. In our secular age, the spiritual poverty all around us is great and cries out for the Bread of Life.

So it would seem logical that, while the priest's ministry is to all, there would be a special recognition of the blessedness of the lowly. A priest should have a deep desire to bless them. However, one need not go to the streets of Calcutta to find poor and suffering people. As Mother Teresa said in her 1994 address at the National Prayer Breakfast, "When I pick up a person from the street, hungry, I give him a plate of rice, a piece of bread. But a person who is shut out, who feels unwanted, unloved, terrified, the person who has been thrown out of society—that spiritual poverty is much harder to overcome."[2] For Mother Teresa, the spiritual poverty of the West was much worse than the material poverty of Calcutta. As secularism sweeps the globe, we priests will have our hands full with the spiritual poverty and hunger for the Word of God everywhere around us.

A Focus on the Spiritual

In Old Testament times, blessings often referred to material prosperity. But the blessings of Jesus are strongly focused on the spiritual world. For example, in the Old Testament book of Job, Job was blessed by God and had a wealth of offspring and material possessions. He had seven sons and three daughters. He had seven thousand sheep, three thousand camels, five hundred yoke of oxen, five hundred she-asses, and more animals besides (see Jb 1:2–3). God pointed out to Satan how faithful Job was. But Satan complained to God that Job was righteous because God had protected him and "blessed the work of his hands" (Jb 1:10).

God handed over Job into Satan's power, and his material blessings were taken away. Job then "cursed his day" (Jb 3:1). But he did not curse God, contrary to Satan's prediction (see Jb 2:5) and also contrary to the advice of his wife, who told him, "Curse God and die!" (Jb 2:9). When his trials ended, with him having shown himself faithful to the Lord even during the time of trial, "the LORD blessed the latter days of Job more than his earlier ones" (Jb 42:12). Now, Job was given even *more* material possessions than before, and thus he was even more richly blessed. He now had twice as many sheep, camels, oxen, and she-asses. He had seven more sons and three more daughters, and he lived to see his grandchildren and great-grandchildren (see Jb 42:12–16).

On the other hand, the blessings offered by Jesus are not focused on material goods. In his Sermon on the Mount, the blessings concern life in the kingdom of God: "Rejoice and be glad, for your reward will be great in heaven" (Mt 5:12). In that kingdom, there will be a future with no hunger or weeping. Those persecuted for Jesus' sake will reap a great reward in heaven (see Lk 6:20–26).

The focus on the spiritual in the New Testament is emphasized in the opening of the Letter to the Ephesians: "Blessed be the God and Father of our Lord Jesus Christ, who has blessed us in Christ with every spiritual blessing in the heavens" (1:3). The letter begins with the traditional Semitic blessing of God, thanking him for all the ways he has graced us. But the author adds that we are thanking God for every "spiritual" blessing; that is, God blesses us by sending us his Spirit.

Moreover, these blessings come to us "in Christ." The author clearly focuses on God's plan of salvation that has been realized in Christ in "the fullness of times" (Eph 1:10). The ultimate blessing of God is the blessing of salvation that comes to us in Christ.

The ultimate blessing of God is the blessing of salvation that comes to us in Jesus Christ.

We see this focus on spiritual blessings, and the greatest of blessings found in God's salvation, in the final judgment. At that time, God will separate people into two groups: sheep and goats. Those on his left, the goats, will be "accursed" (Mt 25:41) because they did not attend to the lowly ones whom Jesus pronounced as blessed: the naked, the hungry, the thirsty, the sick, and those in prison. The ones who ignored the lowly and needy will be cursed and cast "into the eternal fire prepared for the devil and his angels" (Mt 25:41). However, those who cared for the lowly, and thus cared for Jesus himself, will be blessed. Jesus invites them: "Come, you who are blessed by my Father, inherit the kingdom prepared for you" (Mt 25:34).

Here in this gospel story, we again see the scriptural themes of "blessing" and "curse." Those who do the Father's will are blessed, and those who do not are cursed. However, Jesus now changes the focus for the blessing from material rewards in this life to spiritual rewards culminating in salvation. Rather than camels and sheep in this life, the blessed will "inherit the kingdom," and the cursed will be thrown into the "eternal fire."

This shift in emphasis to spiritual blessings in the kingdom does not mean that these blessings are received only in the future. There is, even now, a beginning realization of these spiritual blessings. It is a reflection of a "realizing eschatology"; that is, the kingdom of God has already begun in this life, but it will only achieve its fullness in the next. Thus, the follower of Jesus has already begun to receive the seeds of these blessings: a foretaste of the future fullness of the kingdom.

The blessings Jesus bestows are focused on spiritual realities and the in-breaking of the kingdom into our lives. Even in this life, we begin to taste some of the blessings of the coming realization of the kingdom, such as joy, peace, protection from evil, and a personal relationship with Jesus' Father.

There are many examples of the blessings that, even now, are being bestowed on the disciples of Jesus. These manifold spiritual blessings result from the in-breaking of the kingdom of God in one's life. These blessings are impossible to number. One, for example, is the blessing of joy. Jesus offers to us to share his joy completely (see Jn 17:13). He offers us a peace that the world cannot give (see Jn 14:27). We are protected from Satan and his followers: Jesus prayed to the Father that he "keep [us] from the evil one" (Jn 17:15). Jesus now offers to us his loving relationship with the Father, most explicitly when he gave us that radical address for God, "Our Father" (Mt 6:9). And finally, he said, "I give them eternal life, and they shall never perish" (Jn 10:28).

So when I lay my hands on people's heads in blessings, I often include a spontaneous prayer that they will know God's joy and peace, gifts that Jesus promised his disciples. For those who are troubled, suffering, wounded, or struggling, I include an invocation for their courage, strength, and healing, just as Jesus healed. For those who are feeling unsafe or in need of protection, I pray that God and his holy angels will watch over them. And I end the prayer asking that, one day, the Lord will raise them to the fullness of life in God.

Thus, I am praying that God's kingdom will break into their lives in the way they seem most in need of at that very moment. I trust that God will also give them many other graces of the in-breaking kingdom besides.

MATERIAL BLESSINGS
LEADING US TO SPIRITUAL BLESSINGS

Despite focusing on spiritual blessings, Jesus did not ignore the material world. We humans are both flesh and spirit. Jesus, assuming our humanity, is also both spiritual and material. He too knows and supports our very human needs. But ultimately the spiritual takes precedence.

Jesus often used material blessings to open people up to the greater spiritual blessings. He healed the paralytic after forgiving his sins. Some of the people murmured, saying, "Who but God alone can forgive sins?" (Mk 2:7). Jesus responded, "'But that you may know that the Son of Man has authority to forgive sins on earth'—he said to the paralytic, 'I say to you, rise, pick up your mat, and go home'" (Mk 2:10–11). Clearly the physical healing was in service of a much more important healing: the forgiveness of sins. In the Gospel of John, after Jesus was asked to cure the royal official's son, he said, "Unless you people see signs and wonders, you will not believe" (Jn 4:48).

I have known priests who have a wonderful charism of physical healing. By God's grace, they bring special healing graces, some clearly miraculous, to many people. People are astounded at this and flock to such priests, as they flocked to Jesus. God, in his mercy, draws such people to himself through material blessings.

Of course, all of these people who have been cured will eventually die. But what is of greatest value is the spiritual healing Jesus offers in many ways and often through the hands of his priests. It is these spiritual blessings that are of the greatest importance. "What profit is there for one to gain the whole world and forfeit his life?" (Mk 8:36).

As priests, perhaps some days we wish we could physically heal people, just as Jesus did by merely touching them, especially when we visit the sick. Most senior priests have had isolated instances where they anointed a sick person or prayed over someone who was ill, and they recovered seemingly miraculously or clearly received some sort of special grace. For example, at a funeral reception recently, a young woman asked me for a blessing. She explained that she was going in for cancer surgery the next day. I laid my hands on her head and prayed. She then told me, "I felt something when you blessed me," and she was very grateful. The tumor turned out to be benign, and she is fine.

These isolated manifestations remind us, priests and faithful, what happens with blessings, even though their effects are usually unseen. As we will explore later, priests continue to bless crops, ships, houses, and all sorts of things in this world. This is good. But in the New Testament, the focus on blessings shifts from blessings in this material world to spiritual blessings in this world and in the next. The emphasis shifts from material welfare to grace and holiness. The things of this world are meant to be used rightly as a means to furthering God's saving plan for us and for all of his creation.

What Jesus did, he empowers us priests to do: to bring God's spiritual healing to the world. At times, this healing breaks forth into clear view, and we witness a physical healing or such. But mostly, instead of saving people's mortal lives, we assist God's saving action in their souls. This is the greatest blessing the priest brings from and in Jesus. Whether or not one receives material blessings or physical healings, God always blesses his creation in Jesus.

CURSING OF THE FIG TREE

There is also in the New Testament a continuation of the Old Testament notion of curses. Those who follow God's will are blessed, but those who do not are cursed. As Paul said to the Galatians, "If anyone preaches to you a gospel other than the one that you received, let that one be accursed!" (Gal 1:9).

However, the New Testament shifts the focus to Jesus himself. Those who choose him are blessed, and those who do not are cursed. "Nobody speaking by the spirit of God says, 'Jesus be accursed.' And no one can say, 'Jesus is Lord,' except by the holy Spirit" (1 Cor 12:3). And again, "If anyone does not love the Lord, let him be accursed" (1 Cor 16:22).

Regarding the impending judgment for sin and unfaithfulness, Jesus himself pronounced a prophetic curse. Seeing the barrenness of the fig tree, Jesus cursed the tree: "May no fruit ever come from you again" (Mt 21:19). The fig tree withered and died (see Mt 21:18–22; Mk 11:12–14, 20–25). In Matthew, the tree withered immediately; in Mark, it happened over two days. This curse and the subsequent death of the tree reflect a kind of Old Testament prophetic action. The prophet pronounces a curse, and the words themselves carry a power that actualizes the prophecy. Jesus' action of cursing the fig tree prophesized the coming judgment and punishment for unfaithfulness.

But Jesus strongly centered his actions not on the magical effect of any words but on the power of God. The disciples too will have this authority if they have faith and truly pray (see Mt 21:21–22; Mk 11:22–24). Disciples will even be able to say to a mountain, "Be lifted up and thrown into the sea," and it will be done (Mk 11:23). Disciples who truly have faith and pray, like Jesus, will act in accord with the Father's will. The words they pronounce will carry prophetic power because they ultimately come from God.

We ought to pray much and abandon ourselves to God. When we are united to God, our words are one with the Word. Then, our words and actions enflesh the prophetic power of the Spirit.

Thus, we priests ought to spend much time in daily prayer and also abandon ourselves to God. With assiduous prayer and abandonment to God, our hearts and wills become more completely in sync with Jesus. When we move as one with him, the divine power flows through us more fully. Our words then are in harmony with the Word and carry a prophetic power.

BLESS AND DO NOT CURSE

Perhaps what is most striking about the teaching of Jesus in regard to curses is his raising up the level of discourse into the values of the kingdom of God. When the Christian is cursed by another, Jesus calls upon the Christian to return a blessing. In his teaching on loving one's enemies, the follower of Jesus is called to "bless those who curse you" (Lk 6:28). It is perhaps Jesus' preaching about loving one's enemies that is one of his most remarkable and demanding messages.

Indeed, true disciples of Jesus must love their enemies. There is no place in their hearts for hatred and no room on their tongues for curses.

Thus, anyone in our day who utters a curse on others cannot be acting as a Christian. This ought to serve as a warning to those who engage in the occult practice of trying to punish or bring down calamities on their neighbors.

Sadly, I have heard of occasions where individuals, claiming to be Christians, use occult rituals to curse others.[3] Jesus' teaching roundly condemns it. Not overlooking the possible damage to others, such actions first bring evil upon the practitioner. Anyone who uses evil means will themselves be tainted by the same evil and eventually fall under its sway.

Jesus commands his followers to love their enemies. There is no room in their hearts for hatred. Christians may not curse others but rather are called to return a blessing when they are cursed.

This even applies to simply harboring anger and hatred in one's heart. Harboring hatred in one's heart is tantamount to silently cursing the other person. Do we think that this silent curse has no effect on the other person? I suspect it has a lot more impact than we realize. I am amazed at times at how people do sense the negative judgments and hatreds that others have for them. A brief look in one's eyes or a gesture can convey much more than we realize. Jesus said that the one who is "angry with his brother will be liable to judgment" (Mt 5:22). In fact, 1 John 3:15 goes so far as to say, "Everyone who hates his brother is a murderer." Just as the evil of a curse redounds to the practitioner as well, so too hatred in one's heart eats away and eventually destroys the soul.

In the final consummation of all things in the kingdom, there is no place for anything evil. Nothing accursed will be admitted. As we read in the book of Revelation, describing the New Jerusalem: "Nothing accursed will be found there anymore" (Rv 22:3). Rather, the Lord God will be our light and our joy.

If we, the People of God, wish to enter the kingdom of God, then we will eventually have to be purified of any hatred in our hearts. We must truly love *all* of our brothers and sisters, including terrorists, liberals, conservatives, child molesters, Republicans, Democrats, and the host of others on this planet with whom we might disagree or even loathe, notwithstanding any evil they might have committed. If we "curse" by simply wishing them ill, we have become no better than the evil we eschew.[4]

We must truly be like our heavenly Father, who "makes his sun rise on the bad and the good, and causes rain to fall on the just and the unjust" (Mt 5:45). We must be perfect, "just as your heavenly Father is perfect" (Mt 5:48).

GOD'S NAME IS THE BLESSED ONE

The New Testament clearly continues the Old Testament notion that God is the source of all blessings. God is the source of all that is good. In fact, a New Testament name for God is "the Blessed One." In Mark, Jesus is interrogated by the high priest, who asks, "Are you the Messiah, the son of the Blessed One?" (Mk 14:61). Here, God is referred to as "the Blessed One." In the New Testament, this same title is used *only* in reference to God (*eulogētos*).[5] It is not used as a proper title in reference to anyone else.

It is found in Luke in Zechariah's canticle, "Blessed be the Lord, the God of Israel" (1:68). It is found in the Pauline letters as well, where Paul calls God the one "who is blessed forever" (Rom 1:25). It is echoed in 2 Corinthians: God is "he who is blessed forever" (11:31).

Jesus himself strongly emphasizes this point. When the rich official in Luke 18 addressed him as "Good teacher," Jesus sharply corrected him. He said, "Why do you call me good? No one is good but God alone" (vv. 18–19). Theologians have debated why Jesus rebukes him for calling him "good." Varying interpretations have been given, but it seems likely that Jesus was emphasizing the centrality of God and his goodness.[6] Jesus is not denigrating himself, or us, since any goodness that we have is the presence of the Blessed One in us. But Jesus' life was lived in obedience and praise of his Father.

Apparently, there are increasing numbers of people today attempting to obtain blessings from sources other than God. In Christian theology, this approach is considered a form of magic. This is the problem with modern attempts at witchcraft, even what is called "white witchcraft." All such occult practices, even if not explicitly invoking demonic powers, attempt to obtain blessings or benefits from a spiritual source that is not

God. They are violations of the first commandment to believe and worship the one true God.

God himself is the Blessed One. He is the source of all blessings. Any attempt to obtain graces from other sources, such as the occult or witchcraft, is a violation of the first commandment.

Sadly, one survey in Italy found that in the last five years, more than ten million people contacted 22,000 "magicians." This represents about 20 percent of the population.[7] Such people, including "white witches," often believe they are invoking powers of goodness, but the opposite is likely the case, regardless of how well intentioned these individuals may be. When spiritual forces are invoked and God is not the recipient of the request, it is dangerous.

Jesus Is God's Blessing

As with references to God, in the New Testament the word *blessed* applies to Jesus in a unique way. All four gospels repeat the praise of Jesus as he entered Jerusalem immediately before his crucifixion: "Blessed [*eulogēmenoi*] is he who comes in the name of the Lord" (Jn 12:13).[8] This is a direct citation of Psalm 118:26 and was used of pilgrims entering the holy city.

John the Baptist asked Jesus, "Are you the one who is to come?" (Mt 11:3). Jesus responded by citing the prophet Isaiah and the fulfillment of his prophetic signs. In the gospels, the "one who is to come" is a name uniquely applicable to Jesus.[9] Jesus is the one who comes in God's name in an unrepeatable way.[10]

Given Jesus' unique relationship with the Father, the term "blessed" refers to him in a singular way. Jesus affirmed that he is the true Son of the Blessed One. To the high priest's question, "Are you the Messiah, the son of the Blessed One?" Jesus responded, "I am" (Mk 14:61–62).

Recognizing the perceived "blasphemy," the high priest tore his garments
(see Mk 14:63–64).

We, who are followers of Jesus, recognize him as the true Son of God,
the Messiah, the God-man. As the God-man, Jesus incarnates the Blessed
One. Jesus brings to us the fullness of God's blessings because he himself is
divine and embodies the fullness of the presence of the Blessed One. Thus,
the source of all blessings, God, is now fully present to us.

God's blessings now come to us in their fulfillment and saving
power in Jesus. He is the true Son of the Blessed One.

As Claus Westermann noted, in the New Testament we have a "conscious and emphatic transformation of the Old Testament concept of
blessing."[11] God's blessings now come to us in their fulfillment and saving
power in Jesus. This is especially pronounced in Galatians 3, where Paul
explains the promise made to Abraham: "Through you shall all the nations
be blessed" (v. 8). Thus shall the Gentiles become blessed or, in this case,
offered salvation. Paul saw the fulfillment of this promise of salvation in
Jesus.

The door to realizing these blessings of salvation in one's life is faith.
Paul wrote, "Christ ransomed us from the curse of the law by becoming
a curse for us . . . that the blessing of Abraham might be extended to the
Gentiles through Christ Jesus, so that we might receive the promise of
the Spirit through faith" (Gal 3:14). Again, the teachings of Jesus and the
New Testament smash any possible magical or occult interpretations of
true blessings. We cannot of ourselves conjure up any blessings.

Simon the Magician became a believer but initially clung to his magical
beliefs. He saw the power of the apostles, and he wanted this power for
himself. He offered them money: "Give me this power too, so that anyone upon whom I lay my hands may receive the holy Spirit" (Acts 8:19).
But Peter rebuked him: "May your money perish with you, because you
thought that you could buy the gift of God. . . . Repent of this wickedness"
(Acts 8:20, 22). Previously the scriptures told us that Simon had been

baptized and believed in the Good News. However, it is clear that he had not given up his magical thinking and magical ways. Peter told him, "Your heart is not upright before God" (Acts 8:21). Moreover, Peter added, "For I see that you are filled with bitter gall and are in the bonds of iniquity" (Acts 8:23). This is a stinging judgment, and perhaps we might think Peter exaggerated a bit. But I think not.

In the last couple of years, I have been exposed to several people who claim to be Catholic but are immersed in occult practices, and they see no conflict. Some are consulting the dead. Others are using occult crystals to "keep away demons." Still others are claiming to practice "white witchcraft." Just as Simon the Magician was misguided and, unknown to him, was in the "bonds of iniquity," these people are in dangerous spiritual territory. They claim to be doing God's work, but who is their real father?

Rather, the road to God's blessings is through Jesus. He is "the way" (Jn 14:6). How do we become true followers? Again, through faith. In Galatians we read, "Those who have faith are blessed" (3:9). In fact, Galatians speaks of "the curse of the law" (3:13) and suggests that "all who depend on works of the law are under a curse" (3:10). It is only in Christ Jesus that we find life. As Jesus says, "Blessed is the one who takes no offense at me" (Lk 7:23).

The door to receiving God's blessings is faith. When we have faith in Jesus, we are open to receiving the blessings and gifts God wants to and will bestow on us.

But faith itself is a gift. It is one of God's blessings in the new dispensation of salvation. Simon Peter replied to Jesus' question about his identity with his famous confession of faith: "You are the Messiah, the Son of the living God." Jesus responded, "Blessed are you, Simon son of Jonah. For flesh and blood has not revealed this to you, but my heavenly Father" (Mt 16:16, 17). Again, we see that "blessed" (*makários*) in this context refers to a gift from God; and, in this case, it carries the notion of salvation in Christ. Jesus points out that this blessing to Peter can only come from

God, and it is a sign of divine predilection. It is a sign not only of Peter's faith but also that God has chosen him for a special ministry: "Upon this rock I will build my church" (Mt 16:18).

Then Jesus adds, "Whatever you bind on earth shall be bound in heaven; and whatever you loose on earth shall be loosed in heaven" (Mt 16:19). Jesus gives his authority to Peter and to the Church (see Mt 18:18) to bind and to loose. Biblical scholars debate what that authority specifically constitutes in the scriptures, but the fact that Jesus gave the keys to Peter, and thus a special authority, is not disputed.

In the light of many other scripture passages, it is clear that Jesus passed on his power to his disciples. In Mark 3:14–15 we read, "He appointed twelve . . . to preach and to have authority to drive out demons." This power cannot be wielded as one arbitrarily wishes. As we saw in the Old Testament, a prophet's words were effective because the will of God was transmitted through them. So too, when the Church binds and looses, it must do so in harmony with the will of God.

This has practical ramifications in blessing. As priests, we ought to be spiritually awake and try to respond when the Spirit would have us offer a blessing. As I go through my day, it seems that God puts people in my path that he intends I should bless. Sometimes I miss the opportunity because I am too distracted, too obsessed with my own busyness, or too focused on my errand at hand.

As priests, we need to be awake to anyone or anything God wishes us to bless during the course of the day. These Spirit-inspired moments are easy to miss if we are distracted or caught up in our own busyness.

A good spiritual exercise for priests is to see each person who comes into their path during the day not as a distraction but as part of God's plan—even if we have another goal in mind. Let us not miss the opportunity to offer God's blessings and to sanctify the world around us, as we are charged to do.

Jesus Blesses the Children

In addition to ministering to the suffering outcasts, Jesus singled out children for a special blessing. It is striking that of all the types of people that Jesus encountered, the New Testament gives a special focus to Jesus' blessing of children. He clearly went out of his way to give them personal blessings.

Pope Francis reminds me of Jesus in this regard. One of the stories among the priests in the Vatican is that if you want to get the pope to notice you in a public audience, show up with a child or person with special need. This pope, like John Paul II and other popes before him, makes a beeline toward these people. He often stops the motorcade so that he can hold a child or bless someone in a wheelchair. His response to them is immediate and instinctive. I suspect the Vicar of Christ got this from Jesus himself!

Jesus' encounter with the children is one of the few times he upbraided his own disciples in public. Just as parents hold up their babies for the pope to touch and embrace, parents brought their children to Jesus. As the scriptures recount, "People were bringing children to [Jesus] that he might touch them" (Mk 10:13). When the disciples tried to keep the children away, Jesus became "indignant"—a strong reaction for sure. Then Jesus "embraced them and blessed them, placing his hands on them" (Mk 10:14–16).

What was it that the children received from Jesus in this blessing? This is a profound question and a difficult one to answer. Such a question begs us to "label" and "reify" grace, which is ultimately beyond human capacity. One solid answer is found in the thought of theologian L. Brun: "His blessing and the laying on of hands impart to the children in some way the kingdom itself."[12]

In Jesus' encounter with the children, he gives a model for us who bless in the name of the Church he founded. Certainly we priests are available to bless all of God's people, of whatever faith. To receive a priest's blessing, one need not be Catholic (see Code of Canon Law, no. 1170).

For example, as a chaplain to a professional sports team, I minister to all the players, coaches, and staff. I do not hesitate to give a blessing to an injured player, regardless of his faith. Some of the players most desirous of such a blessing from a priest and most grateful for it are non-Catholics!

To offer a priestly blessing can be a gentle moment of evangelization for non-Catholics as well as for Catholics not practicing the faith.

Blessings can be offered to anyone, Catholic or non-Catholic. Blessings might be said to impart a grace of the kingdom itself.

But the actions of the Master suggest a special focus for priestly blessings: the children as well as the suffering and the poor. For these, we in the Church have a special love and a preferential option. Indeed, Jesus' message suggests that for blessings to be fully effective, the recipient must receive them like a child. God's blessings are most fully received by that part of us that is poor, weak, or childlike. "For the kingdom of God belongs to such as these" (Mk 10:14). Jesus goes so far as to say that if we do not accept the kingdom of God and the blessing of God (that is, accept Jesus, who is the blessing of God) like children, then we will not inherit it at all (see Mk 10:15).

These actions of Jesus imply the most intense of criticisms not only for those who would keep the children away from Jesus but most especially for those who would harm a child. The "curse" that Jesus pronounces is sobering: "It would be better for him if a millstone were put around his neck and he be thrown into the sea than for him to cause one of these little ones to sin" (Lk 17:2). The very antithesis of the priestly call to the blessing of children is abusing them. This is why Pope Francis compared child abuse to "celebrating a black mass."[13] It is an action that is evil and corrupts God's blessings.

It is worth noting that, in the act of blessing, Jesus laid his *hands* on the children. Jesus laid his hands on many people in the act of healing. In the Gospel of Luke we read, "At sunset, all who had people sick with various diseases brought them to him. He laid his hands on each of them and cured them" (4:40).

We also read in Acts about the act of consecrating something to the Lord—that is, "blessing" it—with the same gesture of a laying on of hands. The first "deacons" were set aside for the Lord's service in this way. "They presented these men to the apostles who prayed and laid hands on them" (Acts 6:6). These gospel passages present us with a model of a blessing: prayer and the laying on of hands.

These imply a kind of physical transmission of grace through touch. This is even more explicit in 2 Timothy. Paul reminds Timothy "to stir into flame the gift of God that you have through the imposition of my hands" (1:6). This notion echoes 1 Timothy: "Do not neglect the gift you have, which was conferred on you through the prophetic word with the imposition of hands of the presbyterate" (4:14). In this case, the laying on of hands includes a blessing (named here as the "gift of God") but also the entrusting of an order, a ministry. It is clear that a real grace is transmitted through this blessing. It is not merely an external sign of a grace received in another way. Rather, Paul said the grace was transmitted through the very act of blessing. Moreover, there is an underlying notion of the sacramental nature of the created world, since it is through visible signs that the blessing is imparted.

The gospels give us a model for blessing. A person with authority from God confers the blessing through prayer and a visible sign such as the Sign of the Cross or the laying on of hands.

These scriptural principles are important for a scripturally based, modern understanding of the nature of the Church's blessings. The essentials of a blessing are all present in these biblical passages. First, the blessing is given by one who is blessed or anointed and thus is given authority to bless. Also, the one imparting the blessing does this through prayer (the Word). And there is typically a physical component to the blessing—in this case, the laying on of hands (implying a sacramental view of creation). In our day, blessings recognized by the Church may be conferred by a designated person through the Word, prayer, the Sign of the Cross, and perhaps the laying on of hands.

Blessing of the Loaves and Fishes

Perhaps the most well-known blessing of Jesus occurred when he blessed and multiplied the loaves and fishes and subsequently consecrated the bread and wine at the Last Supper. Here we see a powerful implementation of a sacramental theology of creation. The "stuff" of the sacrament is blessed, and it is transformed by God's grace.

In the first instance, the blessing of the loaves and fishes, the blessing that Jesus pronounces is slightly different in each of the synoptic gospels. In both Mark (6:41) and Matthew (14:19), Jesus "said the blessing, broke the loaves, and gave them." Here, Jesus likely pronounced a typical Jewish table grace. An example of an "ancient Jewish table grace, recorded in the Mishnah, reads, 'Blessed be you, O Lord our God, king of the world, who cause bread to come forth from the earth.'"[14]

However, in the Gospel of Luke, the blessing is actually pronounced over the bread and the fish themselves. Thus the bread and the fish are the focus of the blessing. "Then taking the five loaves and the two fish, and looking up to heaven, he said the blessing over them" (Lk 9:16). Did Luke misunderstand the Jewish blessing formula, or was the change intentional?[15]

Such questions might arise when we pray the blessing at meals or offer blessings in a variety of other contexts: Are we blessing God (i.e., praising) as the ultimate provider of the bounty (i.e., meal), or are we blessing the object itself (i.e., food)? Or are we blessing the people at the table? Does it make a difference?

When we look at the revised, post–Vatican II *Book of Blessings* versus the older, pre–Vatican II *De Benedictionibus*, the blessings at meals are remarkably similar. In the pre–Vatican II "Blessings at Meals," the priest leads the prayers and then pronounces the well-known, traditional blessing: "Bless us, + O Lord, and these thy gifts which we are about to receive from thy bounty. Through Christ our Lord. Amen."[16] It is interesting that the revised *Book of Blessings*, in the Order for the Blessing Before and After Meals, includes the exact same prayer with more modern language: "Bless + us, O Lord, and these your gifts which we are about to receive from your goodness. Through Christ our Lord. Amen."[17] The revised blessing indicates that the priest or deacon "also makes the sign of the cross over the food," while the laity sign themselves with the Sign of the Cross.[18]

In both the revised *Book of Blessings* and the older ritual "Blessings at Meals," God is praised, the people are blessed, and so is the food.

So, in the case of meals, both the revised and the older rituals indicate that it is both the people and the food that are blessed. One might suggest that God is also blessed in these rituals for his "gifts" through the prayers and versicles in the course of the blessing. Thus, perhaps the answer to the question of what it is that we bless at meals in both the revised and old rituals is the same: all three are blessed. God is praised (blessed), the people are blessed, and so is the meal.

THE LAST SUPPER

The miracle of the loaves and fishes prefigures the Last Supper. Again, a physical miracle is a precursor to a spiritual miracle, like the cure of the paralytic. Jesus multiplies the loaves and the fishes to feed the multitude. This is an aid to our limited human understanding of the great miracle of the Last Supper. In the former he feeds the bodies of several thousand, and in the latter he will feed the souls of countless people down through the centuries. And the grace offered in the Eucharist will be a taste of the kingdom itself.

The synoptic gospel accounts and the Pauline account in 1 Corinthians of the Last Supper are all strikingly similar. Jesus took, blessed, broke, and gave (see Mt 26:26; Mk 14:22; Lk 22:19; 1 Cor 11:23–24). In this Passover meal, Jesus transforms the ancient Jewish blessing prayer. Perhaps in the most profound transformation of the Old Testament notion of blessing, the blessing that Jesus pronounces at the Last Supper when taking the bread and the wine refers back to himself and has strong soteriological implications.

Jesus declares that this is "my body" and this is "my blood" (see Mt 26:26–28; Mk 14:22–24; Lk 22:19–20; 1 Cor 11:24–25). Now the focus is on the person of Jesus himself. This, once again, echoes the New Testament understanding of Jesus as the Son of the Blessed One and as thus uniquely blessed. He presents in human flesh God's presence and complete blessing. This blessed bread and wine now make present the eschatological fullness of God's blessings.

Jesus' blessing at the Last Supper and the pouring out of his body and blood are one unified act with his crucifixion and death, which immediately follow, where he pours out his life for humankind. The blessing that we receive from Jesus is nothing less than the kingdom of God itself, which is identified with the person of Jesus. He is the kingdom of God on this earth, now made present in the transformed bread and wine that he blessed.

When we try to understand what a priestly blessing means, we must look to Jesus and see what his blessings meant. "No disciple is superior to the teacher; but when fully trained, every disciple will be like his teacher" (Lk 6:40). We do as the Master did. He has passed his authority to us. Jesus' words here are particularly relevant: "Whoever believes in me will do the works that I do, and will do greater ones than these. . . . Whatever you ask in my name, I will do" (Jn 14:12–13).

Jesus is God's presence among us and thus the fullness of divine blessings. Just as Jesus blessed those around him, ushering in the kingdom in people's lives in many ways, so now his disciples do the same.

Referring to the blessing of children, as noted previously, theologian L. Brun wrote, "His blessing and the laying on of hands impart to the children in some way the kingdom itself."[19] We might conclude that every blessing uttered in Jesus' name ushers in the kingdom of God in some way. It might be a modest way, such as when blessing someone's new house, which is a sacramental. It can also be in a much more profound way, in the Eucharistic sacrament, when the priest blesses the bread and wine at Mass. Each of these has implications for making the kingdom of God present. Each of these has implications for the ultimate salvation of souls. Each of these continues the work and presence of Jesus.

Perhaps what ought to strike us most profoundly is the transformed power of the act of blessing in the New Testament. In Old Testament times, words were understood to carry an innate power. They were not to be uttered frivolously. When people cursed, people might indeed be cursed, especially if the one uttering the words had a prophetic power and election from God. Similarly with blessings, when a holy person blessed another, or a father blessed a child, a grace was indeed offered.

But with the coming of Jesus, the full power of the divine Word is now made present. Jesus *is* the Word of God. When a blessing is uttered in Jesus' name by one given his authority, the grace imparted has ultimate significance. God's Word contains all divine power.

Faith is a critical element in effecting this transmission of grace. When one has faith merely the size of a little mustard seed, mountains can be moved. As Simon the Magician found out, any grace that is imparted must be in conformity with God's will and cannot be manipulated solely by human means. When the priest lives in greater and greater harmony with God's will, when his faith and connection to God are solid, then he can discern when God is ready to impart a special blessing.

Does this mean that the incidents of our blessing people will be rare? Are these unusual moments when God wants us to bless someone? On the contrary, I think that we are stingy with blessings! Our generous God is waiting to pour out divine blessings in abundance on the people—"a good measure, packed together, shaken down, and overflowing" (Lk 6:38). It is we who are frustrating God's generosity at times because we miss the many moments in each day when a blessing, a grace, is needed.

Our generous God is waiting to pour out divine blessings in abundance on the people. We priests likewise ought to be generous in offering these blessings in a myriad of places and situations throughout our day.

We ought never be afraid to ask, "Would you like to receive a blessing?" In several decades of priesthood, I recall few moments when someone has said no. In reality, I think I have neglected many opportunities when God wanted to bless someone and I missed the moment. Brothers, extend your hands over God's people and bless them. At the very least, a "little" grace of the kingdom will be imparted. But it is more likely that we will be astounded at the power of God that flows through the hands of one who ministers in Jesus' name, *in persona Christi capitis.*

4.

A HISTORY OF
BLESSINGS IN
THE CHURCH

Then he led them [out] as far as Bethany, raised his hands,
and blessed them.

—Luke 24:50

EVOLUTION OF SACRAMENTALS

Blessings in themselves are not sacraments, but rather they are called *sacramentals*. The Seven Sacraments (*CCC* 1210) instituted by Christ are "powerful means of salvation" (*LG* 11). They often are associated with the important moments in a person's life, as is the case with Baptism, Confirmation, Marriage, Holy Orders, and the Anointing of the Sick. Of course, the sacraments of Penance and Eucharist are received more frequently. Starting with Baptism, sacraments begin and increase the life of sanctifying grace, which is a habitual state that conforms us to God and frees us to participate in the divine life (*CCC* 1999, 2000).

Sacramentals, on the other hand, are "sacred signs which bear a resemblance to the sacraments" (*CCC* 1667). Sacramentals include blessings, crucifixes, rosary beads, holy water, scapulars, relics of saints, and the like. They are instituted by the Church, and their "effects are obtained through the intercession of the Church" (*CCC* 1667). Sacramentals "do not confer the grace of the Holy Spirit the way that sacraments do" (*CCC* 1670), but rather they can offer graced spiritual effects to help us live out our baptismal calling.[1] Sacramentals can be used to sanctify the daily lives of Christians, and "there is hardly any proper use of material things which cannot be thus directed toward the sanctification of men and the praise of God" (*SC* 61).

In the early days of Christianity, there was no clear understanding of what constituted a sacrament or a clear delineation between sacraments and sacramentals. Living in the late fourth and early fifth centuries, St. Augustine was one of the first to speak of sacraments as "sacred signs," but he did not limit the phrase to mean the Seven Sacraments as we now know them.[2] Rather, they included in addition to the sacraments a variety of holy objects and prayers, which are now called sacramentals.[3] "St. Augustine counted the font of baptism, the giving of salt during baptism, the ashes at baptism, the Lord's Prayer, and Easter Sunday itself as sacraments."[4]

Later, there followed a distinction between *sacramenta maiora* and *sacramenta minora*—that is, major and minor sacraments. By the mid-twelfth century, theologian Peter Lombard and others recognized only seven sacraments that were said to have come directly from Jesus Christ.[5] Eventually, with the Council of Lyons (1274), we have a delineation of the Seven Sacraments, which were later codified in the sixteenth-century Council of Trent.[6]

A blessing is considered a sacramental and not a sacrament. The distinction is often made between the sacraments as being instituted directly by Jesus and the sacramentals as being actions of the Church pointing to and proceeding from the sacraments themselves.[7] This distinction is, of course, not without merit. However, as Rev. Philip Weller pointed out in his introduction to the Roman Ritual's *The Blessings*, there are sacramentals that were clearly instituted by Christ, such as the washing of the feet.[8] One could easily add blessings to that. Jesus blessed people. He blessed children. He blessed his disciples. He also blessed the sick.

Sacramentals have a long and important role in the Church. Their significance has been underlined through the centuries. Among all the sacramentals, Church blessings carry a special importance. The *Catechism of the Catholic Church* reads, "Among sacramentals, blessings (of persons, meals, objects, and places) come first" (*CCC* 1671). Nevertheless, the sacramentals are "extensions and radiations of the sacraments" themselves and point to the centrality of the Seven Sacraments.[9]

Sacramentals have a long history of importance in the lives of the faithful. Sacramentals are "extensions and radiations of the sacraments." First among the sacramentals are blessings.

It is time for us to rediscover the often-hidden power of the Church's blessings. While not sacraments themselves, they are integral parts of the sacraments. What sacrament does not include a blessing? For example, the *Order of Celebrating Matrimony* includes a solemn nuptial blessing. Its words remind us of the Old Testament understanding of the blessing that children are: "May they be blessed with children . . . who live to see their children's children."[10] In the sacrament of Penance, the penitent typically begins, "Bless me Father, for I have sinned." The celebration of Baptism is filled with blessings of water and people and a minor exorcism. One cannot separate blessings and the sacraments; their existence is intertwined.

While we would not say that a blessing of itself, when separated from a sacrament, can bestow sanctifying grace, perhaps a faith-filled pastoral encounter, culminating with a priestly blessing, could become by God's mercy and grace a salvific moment. While sacramentals are not necessary for salvation per se, they are an important part of the believer's saving journey.

We have seen in the previous discussion on blessings in the New Testament that blessings are thought to bestow a grace of the kingdom. Could one imagine a scenario in which a dying person, reaching out in hope to a priest for a blessing, might receive a saving grace? There is no doubt in my mind that it has happened on more than a few occasions.

The Liturgical Blessings at the Beginning and End

The word *blessing* is used of many different acts and in many different contexts. For example, blessings can be a liturgical act as contained in the *Book of Blessings*. They can also be a genre of prayer and intercession found in the sacraments themselves. For example, the parting blessing at the end of the Mass comes down to us from an ancient tradition. When people in these ancient cultures left each other, they would bid farewell and offer a blessing in the name of God. In our secular day, this might seem odd or overly pietistic. But in the ancient world, which had not yet been desacralized, all of life and creation was infused with God's presence.

It is only recently that we have lost a sense of the sacramentality of the world. For example, one way still to say goodbye in Spanish is *vaya con Dios*, which literally means "go with God." In fact, *goodbye* itself is a contraction of "God be with you." When learning Spanish, I found it odd that people in the language class did not realize exactly what they were saying with *vaya con Dios*. They knew it meant "goodbye" but did not grasp what the words actually meant. It was common practice in the ancient world for the person leaving someone's company to be blessed by the one remaining.

And so it is at the end of the liturgy, the people are sent off with a blessing. The blessing at the end of worship now carries a special significance since the event that is being concluded is a sacred event, and thus the blessing has a clear sacred meaning. The people are moving out of the dedicated, sacred space and are sent forth with God's blessing and protection. As Claus Westermann pointed out, this blessing is a bridge for the people between the sacred assembly and the external world.[11]

Westermann has also noted that the opening greeting in the liturgy, "The Lord be with you," and the final blessing go together like bookends.[12] The opening greeting is itself a form of blessing. In the ancient world, this initial greeting was given reciprocally. When meeting each other, two Hebrew people would exchange a blessing. One would say, "The Lord be with you," and the other would respond, "The Lord bless you."[13] In our modern liturgy, this reciprocal blessing is echoed: "The Lord be with you" is followed by "And with your spirit." This follows the ancient world, when each would bestow a blessing on the other when first greeting each other.

However, the final blessing was not reciprocal, as the one who was leaving was traditionally only blessed by the other.[14]

The ancient blessings in greetings and leave-taking have now become bookends in our sacramental encounters. Blessings are an integral part of every sacrament.

Our modern liturgical form has continued this ancient form of blessing in greeting and leave-taking and infused it with a sacred significance. The stuff of this world, already sacred having been created by God, is taken up into the Christian dispensation and transformed in Christ. We take water and baptize. We take bread and wine, and it becomes the Body and Blood of Jesus. Oil from the olive is blessed by the bishop and used to anoint the sick. The stuff of this world is "blessed," and it is imbued with a special holy significance. The ancient blessings in greetings and leave-taking have now become the bookends of our sacramental encounters.

THE BLESSING OF THINGS

An important discussion is whether or not "things" should be blessed. The faithful have a long tradition of asking priests to bless objects. Historian Derek Rivard has suggested that the concept of blessed objects evolved from the developing understanding of sacraments. As sacraments were considered a combination of matter and form, people then began to believe that the matter in the sacraments was itself holy and could be a source of grace. Thus, the water and oil used in sacraments came to be viewed as holy. This eventually led to an understanding that other objects may be blessed as well.[15]

In our own day, priests bless houses, cars, ships, fields, water, and a seemingly unlimited range of things. The *Catechism of the Catholic Church* recognizes and endorses this pious practice: "Among sacramentals blessings (of persons, meals, objects, and places) come first" (*CCC* 1671). It is taken for granted that the Church will bless not only people but also "meals, objects, and places."

A clear confirmation of this teaching occurs every Wednesday morning in St. Peter's Square. At the end of the papal audience, in several languages, the faithful are encouraged to hold up their religious articles, and the Holy Father blesses them. Priests and people bring these blessed rosaries and other religious objects home and pass them out to their parishioners and friends, saying, "This has been blessed by the pope!" The response is typically one of excitement to have such a holy object. It was not only blessed but it was also blessed by the pope himself!

The *Catechism* gives a rationale for blessings: "Every blessing praises God and prays for his gifts" (*CCC* 1671). This recovers the Old Testament notion of blessing as the praise of God, and it also invokes a blessing from God as well, since we are praying for "his gifts." But there is some question raised in theological circles about whether objects in themselves should be blessed or if they are blessed simply in their use by human beings in accord with God's plan of salvation. As we shall see, in the liturgical reform in the wake of Vatican II, which informed the revised *Book of Blessings*, "In blessings of objects the prayer is not over the object in question but relates to the human beings who use the object."[16]

The blessing of things actually started early in the Church's history. As historian Derek Rivard noted, "Blessings are present in the earliest liturgical documents surviving from the postapostolic era of the Church's history."[17] The blessing of things was first associated with objects related to the sacraments.[18] For example, the water used in baptism was itself blessed. Around AD 256, St. Cyprian of Carthage wrote: "It is required then that the water should first be cleansed and sanctified by the priest, that it may wash away by its baptism the sins of the one who is baptized."[19] In the fourth century, the bishop of Thmuis, St. Serapion, included a blessing of oil and water in his sacramentary for bishops. In the *Euchologion of Serapion of Thmuis*, the practice of blessing the water of baptism was extended and applied to blessing water for pious use outside of baptism.[20] Initially there were few blessings of objects, and these were done in the context of the Eucharist. As the number of blessings expanded to include other objects and events, they were blessed in separate liturgical celebrations.[21]

In the third-century *Apostolic Tradition*, sometimes ascribed to Hippolytus of Rome, there is a blessing of first fruits of the field.[22] But it states, "Only certain fruits may be blessed," including pomegranates, figs, grapes, olives, pears, apples, mulberries, peaches, cherries, almonds, and plums. Interestingly enough, the document explicitly states, "Not the pumpkin, nor the melon, nor the cucumber, nor the onion, nor garlic."[23] Similarly, roses and lilies could be offered and blessed as first fruits but not other flowers.[24]

These gifts would be offered to the bishop, who would then pray a blessing prayer: "We give thee thanks, O God, and we offer thee the first-fruits; which thou has given us to enjoy . . . for the gladness and the food of men and all beasts. For all these things we praise thee, O God."[25] This prayer of blessing, perhaps reminding us of the Jewish *berakah*, praises and thanks God for his gifts. These fruits are given by God to "men and all beasts" for their food.

"Every blessing praises God and prays for his gifts." There is a long history in the Church of blessing objects, even up to today with the pope blessing religious articles at the weekday audiences.

Down through the centuries, the blessing of things expanded to a wide range of objects used in daily life, such as seeds, farms, fields, and ships. Blessings also included a variety of situations in life that were not specifically blessed in a formal sacrament, such as the blessing of expectant mothers and the enthronement of kings and queens.[26]

Not long ago, I was driving through southern Maryland and noticed a sign that read, "50th Annual Blessing of the Fleet, October 1." It turns out that the oyster-harvesting season begins in early October. Each year, for the last fifty years, a Catholic priest has been invited to bless the oyster boats. The tradition began with Fr. John Madigan, pastor of Holy Angels Church in Avenue, Maryland. He suggested to the District Optimist Club an annual event to bless the boats as the harvest season began. The event typically is now well attended, and I suspect many come for the food, the beer, and the fireworks. But I also suspect that the religious significance of such an event is not lost on some, especially the seamen. Right under the big headlines announcing the festival were the words "Catholic Mass

Celebrated," and next to a photo of the lighthouse was a photo of a huge cement cross.

When a priest blesses an oyster boat, what is he actually doing? Is he blessing the people who will use the boat? Is he blessing (or thanking) God who is the provider of the boat and its crew? Is he requesting that all be kept safe from storms and every evil while using the boat? Is he praying that the people will use the boat in accord with God's will? Is he asking that the boat's mission will be successful in catching oysters? Perhaps it is a bit of all these things.

The blessing of ships was documented in the Latin tradition as early as the eighth century but appeared even earlier in the Greek Church. Blessings for ships in the Latin tradition have included prayers for safe travel and good weather, blessings of the mariners, a blessing of the boats and the nets themselves, prayers for a bountiful catch for fishermen, and protection from "adversaries."[27]

At times, the theology of blessing objects has been unclear and debated by some. There is an ongoing tension between responding to requests for objects to be blessed and the fear of promoting superstition. As we shall see, these are important questions because differing answers to such questions inform the old ritual and the revised *Book of Blessings* and, ultimately, Church practice surrounding blessings.

But underneath all such questions is the Church's consistent conviction that all of creation participates in God's plan of salvation. The greatest blessing for any part of creation would be its sharing in salvation history mediated through Christ. Our ancient practice of blessings implicitly, and sometimes explicitly, recognizes this context and presents it to us in word and gesture.

BLESSING WEAPONS OF WARFARE

There are times when the blessing of things has the potential to be misused. I recently saw a website that said, "Orthodox priests will bless anything," and it showed photos of priests blessing a wide range of things, including rifles, tanks, and fighter planes. The revised *Book of Blessings*, in the section on an Order for a Blessing to Be Used in Various Circumstances, states, "It is not fitting to turn every object or situation into an occasion for celebrating a blessing (for example, every monument erected no matter what its theme, the installation of military weapons, frivolous events)."[28]

Blessing weapons of war is not new. In the tenth-century Romano-Germanic Pontifical, there is a prayer for the blessing of a knight's sword:

> Hearken to our prayers we entreat, Lord, and may you deign by the right hand of your majesty to bless this sword, with which this your servant N. desires to be girded about, in so far as it can be the defense and protection of churches, widows, orphans and all of those serving God, against the ferocity of the pagans, and may it be dread, terror and fear for others laying snares.[29]

In Old Testament times those who fought in holy wars were automatically consecrated to God. Similarly, the medieval knight was thought to have a sacred role in defending the faith and sacred places. It is important to note that the blessing of his sword was intended to direct the knight to a proper use of the weapon in defense of the defenseless and in the service of God and the Church.

In 1981, there was an outcry from the Catholic Church in the United States with the launching of a new nuclear-powered attack submarine named *Corpus Christi*. The Senate Armed Services Committee spokesperson said the intention was to name the submarine after the city in Texas (Corpus Christi). Apparently they had not considered the actual meaning of the name of the city (Body of Christ). Jesuit theologian Fr. Richard McSorley asked, "We call [the sub] *Corpus Christi*. . . . Do we think God feels honored by it?"[30]

One could perhaps justify blessing a knight's sword to be used for defending "widows, orphans" and for the "protection of churches" in the Middle Ages, but blessing a nuclear-powered submarine in modern times and endowing it with the name *Corpus Christi* is seen by many in the Church as beyond the pale. This would be particularly true if the submarine carried nuclear weapons, given the Church's recent statements on nuclear weapons. This includes Pope Francis's 2017 letter to the United Nations calling for the elimination of all nuclear weapons. Bishop Drury of the Diocese of Corpus Christi and all 270 US bishops at their annual meeting denounced the use of the name *Corpus Christi* since the submarine "has the potential for massive destruction."[31]

Would it be appropriate today to bless other weapons of war that are not weapons of mass destruction? Modern weapons can be explicitly brutal and lethal. One could understand why a Catholic priest might have a problem blessing a two-thousand-pound bomb, an armored tank, or a cruise missile.

Not everything or every situation is suitable for a blessing.

Nevertheless, the service and sacrifices of our military personnel in the defense of the nation and its democracy are laudatory. Moreover, the role of our military chaplains is praiseworthy, and some have been examples of heroic virtue. Such is the case of Fr. Vincent Capodanno, Servant of God, who died in Vietnam ministering to the wounded under intense enemy fire.[32] He was posthumously awarded the Congressional Medal of Honor, and his cause for sainthood is being pursued. It is interesting to note that the USS *Capodanno*, a fully armed destroyer escort named after him, received a documented papal blessing in 1981 from Pope John Paul II. The document stated, "The Holy Father John Paul II paternally imparts his Apostolic Blessing for the USS Capodanno . . . on the occasion of the fourteenth anniversary of the death of Father Vincent Capodanno."[33]

The *Catechism* suggests that blessings not only praise God but also offer the "Church's intercession for men that they may be able to use God's gifts according to the spirit of the Gospel" (*CCC* 1678). The blessing for a knight's sword emphasized that the blessing was for its proper use, and thus the blessing was first directed at the user of the sword. The blessing was for the knight to use his sword in accordance with holy purposes. The same might be said of the documented papal blessing of the USS *Capodanno*.

Blessing our soldiers, sailors, and airmen would clearly be encouraged, as witnessed by Fr. Capodanno, who gave his life to help the wounded. One can understand the Church blessing weapons of war in order that they might be used for a just cause and employed rightly by those wielding such weapons. Whether one would actually bless the bombs and bullets themselves would be something more likely to give pause to our priests—and rightly so.

SACRAMENTALITY OF CREATION

One of the concerns in blessing objects themselves is that it has the potential to lend itself to magic. This was the criticism of German theologian Reiner Kaczynski, who wrote, "The idea that there was magic at work inevitably grew as soon as bishops and priests gave blessings privately without any participation of the people."[34] Thus, as the priest blessed objects privately, some liturgists like Kaczynski viewed the act as lending itself to a kind of magical interpretation—that is, as if the priest had a special magical power to affect the object itself.

In order to face this question squarely, and thus the nature of blessings themselves, one needs to look closely at the Church's theology of creation. The first question we must address is this: Does creation have an intrinsic value of its own outside of the human person, or is its worth directed solely at the human person?

When reading the book of Genesis, one might conclude that all of creation is under the dominance of the human person and that its function is to serve us. Indeed, we read in the book of Genesis that we are to "subdue" the earth and to have "dominion" over "all the living things." Moreover, we are given the plants and trees and fruit for our food. After all, the rest of creation was deemed to be "good," but when the human person was created, God found man and woman to be "very good" (1:28–31). Therefore, if the rest of creation's role is to serve the human person, then does it make sense to bless anything else but people? Thus objects are to be "blessed" only in their relationship to people.

However, I believe that when we posit that the rest of creation is here only to serve us, it can become a form of modern anthropocentrism where we place ourselves as humans at the center and apex of all things. In this view, the rest of creation only serves us; this has the potential to lead us into doing what we will with it, to include draining and ultimately destroying it for our own designs. As Pope John Paul II noted in *Redemptor Hominis*: "Man often seems to see no other meaning in his natural environment than what serves for immediate use and consumption."[35] Pope Francis likewise condemns such an attitude in his encyclical *Laudato Si'*: "Clearly, the Bible has no place for a tyrannical anthropocentrism unconcerned for other creatures."[36]

We ought to be reminded that the human person is not the center of creation. God is the center of all things, including creation. While we are given dominion over creation, it means we are to nurture and actually serve the good of all creation. For Jesus, as we learn from the New Testament, to exercise authority means to humbly serve others' needs and to care for them. Such is the vision behind Pope Francis's encyclical.

In fact, most of creation is, and according to some scientists will always be, outside of our grasp and even outside of our vision. The Hubble Telescope has given us a magnificent view of only a minuscule piece of this vast, beautiful universe. We are told that it is ever expanding, and thus most of the universe's light may always be beyond our reach. The majority of the universe will likely always be beyond our domination and will never serve us.

But creation can and does fulfill its primary mission—to praise or bless God. Human beings are made in God's image most directly. But in a lesser way, all of creation must have been formed in its Creator's image. The Artist's reflection is in each and every one of his works. In a real way, creation's very beauty praises the Creator who made it. He is the source of all beauty and truth. By its very existence, creation itself sings its own hymn to God.

Such sentiments are echoed in the scriptures. Psalm 19 begins, "The heavens declare the glory of God; the firmament proclaims the works of his hands" (v. 2). The beauty of creation is a silent witness to the glory of God. Again, we read in Daniel 3 the hymn of the three young men who were miraculously saved after being thrown into the furnace: "Sun and moon, bless the Lord. . . . Stars of heaven, bless the Lord. . . . Every shower and dew, bless the Lord. . . . All you birds of the air, bless the Lord" (vv. 62–64, 80).

Perhaps most famous is St. Francis's Canticle of Brother Sun and Sister Moon. In it he wrote, "Praised be You, my Lord, with all Your creatures, especially Sir Brother Sun. . . . Praised be You, my Lord, through Sister Moon and the stars. . . . Praised be You, my Lord, through our Sister Mother Earth."[37] Such personifications of creation and the poetic language can disguise the depth of the theology behind it. St. Francis's vision reminds us of the scriptures in which God declared all of creation good. Creation is a reflection of the beauty of its Creator, and so it silently praises him.

All of creation reflects its Creator and is sacred. All of creation offers its silent praise to God.

One of the geniuses of Catholic theology is its recognition of the inherent graced nature of all creation and ultimately its sacramentality in Christ. All of creation was made through the Word. As the prologue of John's gospel tells us, "All things came to be through him" (1:3). Thus, creation is inherently sacred since it was created by the Blessed One.

Theologian Kevin Irwin has written eloquently about the sacramentality of creation as fundamental for our understanding of the liturgy and sacraments. He pointed out, "We do not live in 'two different worlds,' the sacred and the secular." Rather, "We live in a sacramental world and it is through the liturgy's use of the things of this world that we experience particularly 'strong moments' of God's self-disclosure."[38] Thus, we must take "seriously 'daily and domestic things,' for these are the tangible ways and means the Church uses to experience and partake in the life of God both in liturgy and sacraments and outside of them in all of life."[39]

Each of us priests has heard more than a few people excuse their presence from Sunday communal worship by saying, "I find God in nature." In fact, we all should find God in nature: he is there! However, the New Testament would suggest that we should find God most especially in the Sunday Eucharist, the source and summit of the Christian life (*LG* 11; *CCC* 1324). We find him most directly in the blessing and breaking of the bread, as did the disciples on the road to Emmaus.

A critical insight in forging a theology and pastoral practice of blessings and, in particular, the blessings of creation is to recognize the sacramentality of all that God has made. Creation is not simply a tool for humans, but it has its own inherent worth from its Creator. Pope Francis's *Laudato Si'* and the writings of popes before him underline our duty toward the world over which God has given us dominion. It is a dominion of service, not domination, and it is a dominion of nurturing, not destruction.

THE FALL OF CREATION

But the story does not end with the sacredness of creation. The story does not end with its original pristine beauty. There is a temptation to view creation only from the lens of its initial creation and not from its subsequent history. Creation itself participates in the drama of salvation history.

Creation was initially conceived as a garden called Eden. The word "Eden" comes from the Sumerian word meaning "fertile plain." A similar word in Hebrew means "delight." So one can understand Eden as a "garden of delight."[40]

One might picture the garden before the Fall as a place of tranquility and plenty. The food would be abundant and rich. The weather would always be mild. There would be no strife or conflict either among humans or between them and their natural surroundings. All would be at peace.

But this changed with the sin of Adam and Eve. They were cast out of the garden of paradise. With this sin came specific curses. Eve would bring forth children in pain (see Gn 3:16). Thus there would be pain, exemplified in the birthing of children. Also, creation would no longer be a garden of plenty. Rather, Adam would have to toil for his food. The garden would now become a place where "thorns and thistles" would be his lot (Gn 3:17–19).

Creation itself participates in the drama of salvation history. With the Fall, the garden of paradise yielded to a place of thorns and thistles, pain, conflict, and death.

Genesis tells us that God told Adam, "Cursed is the ground because of you!" (3:17). The earth itself is now cursed because of Adam and Eve's sin. Human beings all fell because of the sin of Adam and Eve. So too did creation fall in some connected way. It was a garden; now it is a patch of thorns and thistles. The ground was cursed.

If the earth has fallen in the wake of sin, then one can see the possibility and efficacy in the Church's blessing of creation. In an agrarian society, people would ask for their seeds, fields, and first fruits as well as anything related to their sustenance to be blessed. This seems wholly appropriate after the reading of Genesis. Human beings were supposed to live in a rich garden, and now they live in a land of thorns and thistles. Any grace from God that might help turn this fallen earth into a fertile garden would be most welcome.

THE REDEMPTION OF CREATION

If creation was made by God to be a garden of peace and plenty and then fell in light of the sin of its custodians Adam and Eve, was it redeemed in Christ? The scriptures suggest that it was. It is worth citing Romans in some depth:

> For creation awaits with eager expectation the revelation of the children of God; for creation was made subject to futility . . . in hope that creation itself would be set free from slavery to corruption and share in the glorious freedom of the children of God. We know that all creation is groaning in labor pains even until now . . . as we wait for adoption, the redemption of our bodies. (Rom 8:19–23)

It is not only human beings who fell, but creation with them. There is an intimate bond between the human person made from "the dust of the ground" (Gn 2:7) and the rest of creation. Now, as St. Paul notes, both humans and all of creation groan together.

Theologian David Power wrote that the blessing of things by the Church was as much a part of the early tradition as was blessing as a thanksgiving to God. Both types of blessing were part of the vision and practice of the early Church. Such blessings reflected "an understanding of sacramental power, that is, the sense that redemption included all creation and that through the things of daily life God mediates protection and love."[41]

Creation is now in "slavery to corruption," St. Paul wrote, but it will "share in the glorious freedom of the children of God." The blessing of animals and objects reflects a sacramental understanding of creation.

These thoughts were echoed by Kevin Irwin: "The world and all who dwell in it are termed 'sacramental,' meaning that the whole cosmos and all that dwell in it are regarded as not only reflecting God's glory but also in need of complete redemption." Thus, Irwin warned us against "becoming too optimistic about the world."[42] And yet we do not yield to pessimism, since in Christ's Paschal Mystery "we are confident in its final perfection."[43]

Just as God makes covenants with human beings, God also makes covenants with other living beings in creation. In Noah's day, after the flood, God made a covenant with Noah and his children and their descendants. But he also made this covenant, through Noah, "with every living creature" (Gn 9:9–10). This is stated a second time in Genesis 9 when God says, "I will remember my covenant between me and you and every living creature" (v. 15). God set the rainbow in the heavens as a sign of protection and covenant with every living being.

The bond between the human person and all of creation is deep. The nature of the human person as both "dust of the ground" and having "the breath of life" when God "blew into his nostrils" (Gn 2:7) is important. When the final age comes and there will be "a new heaven and a new earth" (Rv 21:1), we will not become angels. Rather, our spirits will be reunited with our bodies, although in a transformed state.

A prefiguring of this transformed state occurred in the person of the resurrected Jesus, who walked through walls when he appeared to the disciples in the upper room. The material element of the human person will never be cast aside; our creation from dust is part of who we are. We are forever a part of God's created material world.

Just as the human person will be transformed, body and soul, in the final age, so too will creation be transformed. And there will be a new heaven and a new earth.

Just as the human person will be transformed, body and soul, in the final age so too will creation be transformed. There will be "new heavens and a new earth" (2 Pt 3:13; cf. Is 66:22). This was affirmed in the teaching of the Second Vatican Council: "At that time [at the final restoration of all things] the human race as well as the entire world, which is intimately related to man and attains to its end through him, will be perfectly reestablished in Christ" (*LG* 48). This reemphasizes our duty toward creation. If it is to be taken up into its consummation in Christ, then we must, as its custodians, care for it.

While we cannot completely equate progress on this earth with the new creation, neither can we suggest that harming this planet has nothing to do with impeding its final transformation in the new age. We know that the new heavens and the new earth will inevitably come. Thus, we ought to strive to do all we can to facilitate that, first in the community of human beings and then in our care for the earth.

BLESSING GOD'S CREATION

Thus, human beings participate in redemption and so does creation. Obviously, creation does not have free will, so it cannot choose to sin, although it does suffer the effects of sin, including both original sin and the sins we commit against it. How exactly humans and creation will participate in the new heavens and the new earth is a mystery for us now. But there are scriptural inklings of what is to come.

In Isaiah, the prophet speaks to us of the coming Messianic age when the peace of God's creation will be restored.[44] The violence of this age that began with Cain and Abel is also found in creation. This violence will be healed. "The wolf shall be a guest of the lamb, and the leopard shall lie down with the young goat" (Is 11:6).

The priest blesses creation, imparting a grace of Christ's kingdom, as it participates in the redemption of all things in Christ. Peace and prosperity on the earth may be a sign of the in-breaking kingdom, reversing the violence and barrenness of creation's Fall.

In the new age, "the lion shall eat hay like the ox" (Is 11:7). The Spirit of the Lord will transform all of creation: "For the earth shall be filled with the knowledge of the LORD, as water covers the sea" (Is 11:9). The original peace of the garden of paradise will be restored, and "they shall not harm or destroy on all my holy mountain" (Is 11:9). With the Fall, creation became violent and barren, yielding thorns and thistles. The redemption of creation will right such devastation. Not only will this redemption restore creation's original peace but also creation will be full of the knowledge of the Lord.

As noted earlier, one way of viewing the nature of a blessing is to see it as an in-breaking of the kingdom of God having come to us in Jesus. Surely a sign of this kingdom is a transformation of creation into this idyllic fruitful paradise. Thus it would be more than appropriate to bless a field, praying for it to yield a bountiful harvest. One would surely bless a fishing fleet, praying that it would yield an abundant catch. A priest would be in the right if he blessed the honest labors of any worker lawfully engaged in the right use of God's creation.

A bountiful harvest and productive labors could be viewed by the faithful as a sign of the in-breaking kingdom. In fact, Jesus used just such a sign in the call of Simon the Fisherman. There was a miraculous catch of fish, and Simon exclaimed, "Depart from me, Lord, for I am a sinful man" (Lk 5:8). This material blessing of a miraculous catch of fish was a moment of grace that Jesus used to call Simon to follow him.

It was no accident that the miracle was an abundant harvest of fish. While Jesus could have used a miraculous occurrence of another kind, he used a sign of the in-breaking kingdom appropriate for a fisherman. We priests too might bless any endeavors that can be signs of the in-breaking of the kingdom and a reversal of the tragic effects of sin. In fact, as we bless creation, in a small way we assist in its transformation in Christ as a way of undoing the sin of our first parents. It is hoped that, as the earth yields its harvest and our labors are productive, human beings will be reminded of their Creator, the true Author of all blessings.

It is especially appropriate to bless the labors of men and women, in a reversal of the curse of Adam, and to pray for their fruitful labors and a bountiful harvest. We pray with people that such a blessing might move them to recognize the true Author of all blessings.

In our secular age, fewer may end up stepping into a Church than in the past. So as the priest goes out into the world, often blessing God's creation, these little acts of "redemption" perhaps will lead some to eventually seek out God's great act of redemption presented to us most directly in Christ and the sacraments. As Simon Peter was moved by a miraculous catch of fish, so too might some of God's children be moved by God's grace hidden in the priest's blessings.

The poetic lyricism of St. Francis in his addressing of Brother Sun and Sister Moon is music to our ears. Interestingly enough, the eighth-century Gelasian Sacramentary likewise addresses the water as if it were a living creature: "Wherefore, I bless you, creature of water." This tradition continued until recently with the pre–Vatican II ritual for blessing water. The priest addressed the salt, "Thou creature of salt," and then the water, "Thou creature of water."[45]

This practice was not included in the revised post–Vatican II *Book of Blessings* or in the appendix to *The Roman Missal* for blessing water. While honoring the sacredness of creation and its participation in the redemption of Christ, one can easily argue that addressing inanimate objects directly does not fit into the culture of our times and needed to be adapted. The beauty of poetic lyricism notwithstanding, the revised prayer for the blessing of water rightly addresses God, who is indeed the Author of all blessings.

BEGINNING OF ROGATION DAYS

The ancient tradition of Rogation Days,[46] the blessing of farmers' fields, is an example of the Catholic Church recognizing the importance of blessing God's creation. "Rogation," coming from the Latin *rogare*, means a "request" or "supplication." Replacing pagan traditions of supplicating deities for the welfare of their crops, priests blessed farmers' fields in connection with days of fasting and prayer leading up to the Feast of the

Ascension. Rogation Days often included processions and formal public prayers, such as the Litany of the Saints.

Rogation Days were thought to have become part of the Church's public liturgy in France with Bishop Mamertus of Vienne in the fourth century. It is said that the Diocese of Vienne was beset by diseases, fire, wolves, and earthquakes. The saintly bishop asked for three days of prayers and processions immediately before the Feast of the Ascension. In the wake of these prayers, the afflictions ended. Subsequently, these Rogation Days were adopted by the other French bishops at the Fifth Council of Orléans in AD 511.[47]

Some three hundred years later, Pope Leo III (d. 816) made observing these Rogation Days mandatory as part of the entire Latin Church's liturgy. Their public observance declined subsequently, but in recent years there is increasing interest in this ancient practice.

Blessing of Fields: Old versus Revised

In the pre–Vatican II *De Benedictionibus*, the priest prayed to bless, consecrate, and protect the fields.[48] He sprinkled the land with holy water and made a Sign of the Cross over it, clearly indicating an intention to bless the land itself. In this older Blessing of Fields, blessing the people present was not overlooked. After the Litany of the Saints, the priest prayed "that thou wouldst vouchsafe to snatch from eternal damnation our souls and those of our brethren, relatives, and benefactors."[49]

Reminiscent of ancient prayers against storms, the blessing also included "that thou wouldst vouchsafe mercifully to ward off and dispel from this place all lightning, hail-storm, injurious tempests, and harmful floods."[50] I suspect a farmer, so dependent upon the weather for his livelihood, would be very grateful for such a prayer.

Moreover, in the final prayer of this ritual, the priest prayed that we would have a "sense of constant gratitude for thy gifts."[51] The importance of thanking God is not overlooked in this blessing. So in this Blessing of Fields in the old ritual, we see all three elements of praising God, blessing the people, and blessing the object—in this case, the fields.

In the revised post–Vatican II *Book of Blessings*, the priest or deacon (or lay minister) prays that the land would indeed be protected from "wind and hail" and that it would "be fertile" and yield a "rich crop." There is no sprinkling of holy water indicated or a Sign of the Cross over the land; however, the people are to be blessed with such a sign as the priest prays, "May God, the source of every good, bless + you and give success to your work, so that you may receive the joy of his gifts and praise his name now and forever. Amen."[52] However, such signs of a sprinkling with holy water and a Sign of the Cross are mentioned in the General Introduction and thus presumably may be used.[53]

Again, in the revised rite, we see an emphasis on blessing the people and a moving away from directly blessing inanimate objects. The liturgical reform envisions that the objects are actually blessed precisely because they fulfill their God-given role of assisting people and cooperating in God's plan of salvation. The prayer petitions God that the land "may be fertile with abundant crops" and "then your people, enriched by the gifts of your goodness, will praise you unceasingly."[54] Thus, creation is thought to be graced and blessed when it supports people in praising God for his goodness.

USCCB AND ROGATION DAYS

The US bishops in their letters and instructions have been encouraging a proper stewardship of creation. Certainly this is in keeping with Pope Francis's important encyclical on caring for the environment, *Laudato Si'*. On the United States Conference of Catholic Bishops (USCCB) website, one can find a section, "Prayers to Care for Creation," that includes prayers and liturgies "designed to help parishes incorporate care for God's creation and the pursuit of environmental justice into their prayer and liturgies." Many of these prayers are taken from the revised *Book of Blessings*.[55]

Priests are encouraged by the US bishops to give blessings and to conduct liturgies for the proper stewardship of creation. Pope Francis's *Laudato Si'* teaches us that such stewardship is a critical need in our time to which we are urgently called by God.

The USCCB website currently has some suggested prayers under the heading "Rogation Days: Blessing of Fields and Gardens." The Bishops' Conference indicates that, while Rogation Days were associated with the three days before the Feast of the Ascension, these blessings may now be used any time "when it is appropriate to ask that gardens, fields, and orchards be blessed during the coming season." The service appropriately includes a reading from Genesis 1 about God creating the earth, vegetation, and seed-bearing plants.[56] The Litany of the Saints is included during the procession through the fields, and the following prayer is then said:

> O God,
> from the very beginning of time
> you commanded the earth to bring forth vegetation
> and every fruit of every kind.
> You provide the sower with seed and give bread to eat.
> Grant, we pray, that this land,
> enriched by your bounty and cultivated by human hands,
> may be fertile with abundant crops.
> Then your people, enriched by the gifts of your goodness,
> will praise you unceasingly now and for all ages unending.
> Grant this through Christ our Lord.
> R. Amen.[57]

Reflecting the theology of blessing in Genesis, the priest and people supplicate God to bless the crops and make them fertile. Again, this is a kind of "redemption" of the land that was under the curse of Adam yielding thorns and thistles. As the earth yields its harvest, the context of this prayer might remind human beings not only of God's generosity but also of the redemption of all creation in Christ.

STORMS AND BLESSINGS

An interesting medieval development is the use of blessings for storms. Historian James Monti points out that the earliest known liturgical prayers for deliverance from storms are found in texts from a bishop of Italy (d. 521). In the blessing of the Paschal candle at the Easter liturgy, there is a prayer that the wax from the candle would be a protection against storms "serving as 'an excellent refuge' and a 'wall' against the devil."[58] The faithful would bring home a piece of the wax as a sacramental to be used in protection against storms.

In the eighth century, the Gelasian Sacramentary of Rome included prayers for protection against lightning. Later, in the tenth century, there were full liturgical rites for protection from storms. In a tenth-century liturgical manuscript from Germany, after the Litany of the Saints, the celebrant makes the Sign of the Cross at the clouds and says, "I sign you, O cloud," and adds other invocations including, "O Cross of Christ, which we ever worship, vouchsafe always to be with us against all our enemies."[59] The rite includes the Our Father, the Creed, and the Trisagion, plus Psalm 147, which recalls God as the Lord of creation. There are several exorcistic prayers and a reading from the Gospel of Matthew recounting Jesus' calming of the storm on the sea (Mt 8:23–27).[60]

Jesus' calming of the storm was met with wonder by the disciples: "What sort of man is this, whom even the winds and the sea obey?" (Mt 8:27). It connects Jesus to God, who is the Creator and Lord of all creation. His are the winds and the seas to command. This miracle is just one more sign that Jesus is the true Son of the Blessed One. He is God's presence and the one who redeems humankind and its consequent fallen creation.

Just as the earth's yielding a new fecundity, a new hundredfold, can be a sign of the redemption wrought in Christ, so too the calming of the storm. One can easily see the presence of destructive storms, which often take human life and destroy parts of the earth, as another symbol of humankind's expulsion from the tranquility and peace of paradise. Thus, Jesus' calming of the storm might be seen as a symbol of the redemption of creation. As the Church similarly prays for the calming of storms, we pray, just as Jesus did, that the storms might cease and the tranquility of God's kingdom might ensue. Indeed, it is the Spirit of God that brings order out of the chaos of creation (see Gn 1:2).

It is interesting to note the specific words and actions of Jesus in calming the storm. Jesus "woke up, rebuked the wind, and said to the sea, 'Quiet! Be still!'" (Mk 4:39). In both Mark and Luke, the commands of Jesus to the storm are the same words used earlier in the synoptics in Jesus' exorcizing of the demons. He rebukes the demons and commands them to be still, demonstrating his mastery over them.[61] This was not an accidental use of words. These gospels are clearly treating Jesus' calming of the storm as a kind of exorcism.

This exorcistic element continued in the medieval texts for the calming of storms. A belief in the power of demons to attack a farmer's field and ruin a harvest, cause a blight, or create destructive storms arose early in the Church's history, such as in the writings of Tertullian (ca. 155 to ca. 240).[62] Thus, fields and storms were exorcized and blessed.

A fifteenth-century book of customs from the Archdiocese of Valencia, Spain, stipulated that the church bells should be rung with the approach of a storm. The number of bells used should be in accord with how great the storm is. The bells themselves, having been blessed as objects set aside for sacred use, were thought to have a power in scaring away demons. Of course, the sound of the bells was also used to warn the people of a coming storm and that they should pray for God's protection.[63] The latter steps are no less important!

From Burgos, Spain, there was a rite called Order against Storms, which provided specific rubrics in invoking protection against a storm. The rite stipulates that the priest should be dressed in a surplice and stole. He should open the missal to the Roman Canon, which was thought to have a special power in casting out evil. He was to light the candles and open the tabernacle but leave the Body of Christ inside. The priest should carry the crucifix and relics of the saints as he "exorcized" the storm. In addition to other prayers such as Psalm 30, a prayer of thanksgiving for deliverance, he was to engage in what is now a classic deliverance action by holding up a crucifix and saying "boldly": "Behold the Cross of the Lord; flee, O adverse factions."[64]

Today, if a huge hurricane was on track to devastate a diocese and a local priest stood up on the shore, held up a crucifix, and commanded the demons to depart, he might, if he survived the hurricane, end up in a psychiatric institution. In our secular scientific age, we have a better sense of the science behind storms. The National Oceanic and Atmospheric Administration (NOAA) tracks storms and predicts their intensity, direction, duration, and more. Meteorologists speak about how the warm water can "fuel" a hurricane and make it deadlier. Expert pilots fly into the eye of the hurricane and assist in our understanding of the storm. Indeed, the development of this critical science is one way God helps his people remain safe—through the knowledge gained in the meteorological sciences.

Does it make any sense to bless or exorcize storms anymore? For many it would seem as if we were yielding to fear and superstition. Indeed, we in Christianity do not know specifically if demonic powers actually can directly influence or create destructive weather, nor do we speculate about such things. In recent times, the teaching Church has not officially spoken about such matters.

Secular minds scoff at such seemingly ignorant interpretations, and we ourselves might feel embarrassed even entertaining such an interpretation. But our centuries-old tradition says otherwise, and we ourselves might remain open to the efficacy of blessing and exorcizing a storm before it devastates our city.

For example, the Weller version of *De Benedictionibus* includes prayers for the "Blessing of a Community against Floods" and a "Blessing of a Community to Ward Off Pests."[65] The latter includes an exorcism in the prayers. The revised *Book of Blessings* has a "Blessing to Be Used in Various Circumstances," which includes a prayer option "to ward off every harm."[66] As sacramentals, the prayers can be modified to fit the occasion.

In the face of impending storms and other natural disasters, priests should pray with the people for God's protection and safety.

What is certain in our faith is that God hears our prayers. Divine protection from natural evils in this life is a reflection and a sign of God's protecting us from spiritual evil. We pray for this apotropaic protection every day, as Jesus himself taught us in the Our Father: "Deliver us from evil." It is only God's power in Jesus that definitively delivers us from evil.

God's delivering of his people from natural disasters is as old as Genesis. In this book, God made a special covenant with humankind and all creatures and sealed it with a rainbow. Praying for divine protection in the face of any impending harmful event is a solid part of our biblical tradition.

In fact, in the face of impending disasters including storms, we would be remiss if we Christians did not call out to God for help. And in dire circumstances, I suggest that we priests would be negligent in our duties to the People of God if the Church did not invoke God's help with a prayer and blessing.

5.

THE BOOK OF
BLESSINGS

For he commands his angels with regard to you, to guard
you wherever you go.

—Psalm 91:11

A CALL FOR RENEWAL

The Fathers of the Second Vatican Council called for a renewal of all the
rites of the Church. This included also a renewal of the *Book of Blessings*.
This was much needed. By the time of the Second Vatican Council, *De
Benedictionibus* in the Roman Ritual had become a collection of 179 blessings, of which ninety-five were reserved to bishops or to members of a
religious order. The blessings were uneven and heterogeneous. There was
no clear theology conveyed throughout. The Church had been collecting
them together from a variety of sources over hundreds of years.[1] It was
indeed time for them to be renewed.

In the process of the renewal, what emerged—the new 1984 revised *De
Benedictionibus*—was a significant change from the old collection. Some
commentators felt that this new book benefited from recent advances
in scholarship, especially sacramental theology, and from an attempt to
recover earlier understandings of blessings. In writing the new blessings,
it was felt that some of the medieval accretions to the old blessings should
be downplayed or eliminated altogether.

73

Vatican II's Constitution on the Sacred Liturgy, *Sacrosanctum Concilium*, called for a renewal of the sacramentals along with the sacramental rites of the Church (see *SC* 79). Since a blessing is a sacramental, the principles for the renewal set forth by the Council Fathers were applicable to blessings. These principles included "enabling the faithful to participate intelligently, actively, and easily." As with the sacraments, the Church wanted the faithful to actively participate in these blessings. Also, the previous practice of reserving the majority of blessings to bishops and religious orders was to be changed. For example, the "Blessing and Investiture with Scapular of Our Lady of Mount Carmel" was formerly reserved to Discalced Carmelite priests. The blessing of St. Benedict medals was reserved to Benedictine priests. And the "Blessing of Rosaries of Our Lady" was reserved to Dominican priests. Now, the Council mandated that "reserved blessings shall be very few."

Moreover, in one of the more controversial pronouncements, the Council stated, "Some sacramentals, at least in special circumstances and at the discretion of the ordinary, may be administered by qualified lay persons" (*SC* 79). The latter was justified by tradition since history records that members of the laity were allowed by the Church to bless in certain circumstances. It was also justified by pastoral need. In some missionary regions few priests are available and lay catechists do much of the pastoral and spiritual formation in parishes.[2]

The revised 1984 *De Benedictionibus*, like the older one, did not intend for its blessings to become normative in the same way the rites celebrating the sacraments are normative. Rather, local churches were encouraged to adopt the blessings and adapt them to local needs. The 1989 *Book of Blessings* is the USCCB adaptation of the Holy See's 1984 Latin revised *De Benedictionibus*. The 1989 *Book of Blessings* published in English by the USCCB includes the original orders of blessing from *De Benedictionibus* plus additional orders and prayers composed by the US Bishops' Committee on the Liturgy or from other liturgical books.[3]

Fr. Pierre-Marie Gy, a French Dominican and liturgist, headed the study group on the revision of the *Book of Blessings*. In his April 1970 *relatio*, he presented some of the guiding principles in drafting the new blessings. The primary sources to be used would be the understanding of blessings in the scriptures and the early Church. Thus, the new structure for blessings would be more in line with the Jewish notion of *berakah*. In the Jewish concept of *berakah,* first God is praised and "blessed."[4] Then the blessing extends to God's people.

The Second Vatican Council called for a renewal of all the Church's rites, including blessings. These changes focused on the active participation of the faithful, making reserved blessings few in number, and allowing some sacramentals to be administered by the laity.

Also, Gy said blessings should focus on people and not things. The focus, when blessing objects, should be on the person and the proper use of the object, not on the object itself. Some feared that blessing objects risked stirring superstition in the hearts of the faithful. The consequent concern for not inadvertently promoting superstition became an important consideration throughout the drafting of the new blessings. In the General Introduction to the 1989 *Book of Blessings,* there is a warning against "anything that might replace genuine faith with superstition and/ or a shallow credulity."[5]

Similarly the apotropaic function (that is, warding off evil) was removed in most cases and downplayed throughout, again to guard against what was considered a superstitious misuse of blessings. Sacred objects, for example, ought not to be used as magic talismans.[6] For some centuries prior to the Council there had been an increasing inclusion of the exorcistic functions of blessings, especially those pertaining to holy water. The water was exorcized—that is, any evil presence or influence over the water was cast out—and then the water itself could be used to cast out evil or protect people from it. Those who drafted the new blessings thought that exorcizing water or salt or oil, for example, suggested that such objects were under the control of Satan. In their estimation, this promoted an excessively negative view of creation.

German theologian Reiner Kaczynski wrote that when there was a reference to an exorcistic (casting out evil spirits) or apotropaic function (warding off evil), "a pessimistic view of the world has won out over the biblical understanding of creation as good."[7] (It might be noted that

Kaczynski was appointed as a consultor to the Holy See's Congregation for Divine Worship in 1984 when the revised *De Benedictionibus* was released.)

To reduce any magical notions, the revised blessings focus on blessing God and blessing people rather than blessing objects. The exorcistic function was largely removed. These blessings added a liturgical structure, including readings from sacred scripture and intercessions with responses.

In the revised Order for the Blessing of Holy Water outside Mass, there is no exorcistic function mentioned. Rather, it focuses on using the water to remind us of our baptism. The actual prayer of blessing adds that we may be "refreshed inwardly by the power of the Holy Spirit."[8] On the contrary, in the older pre–Vatican II rite for the Blessing of Oil-Stocks, the priest prays that "these vessels . . . be freed from the contaminating influence of evil spirits."[9] Thus, the older ritual included an exorcistic function of freeing the object from the influence of evil spirits.

Finally, the liturgical nature of blessings and the active participation of the faithful were to be encouraged in the revised blessings. Thus, the revised blessings are meant to be liturgical celebrations with scriptural readings and the active engagement of the laity present. A guiding principle was that "blessings too are liturgical celebrations."[10] Moreover, in the General Introduction to the 1989 revised *Book of Blessings*, the proclamation of the Word of God plus the prayer of blessing are considered to be constitutive of a blessing: "These may never be omitted even when the shorter form of a rite is used."[11]

In the early Church, there were fewer objects blessed as compared with the late Middle Ages, and these early Church blessings were typically done during the Eucharistic celebration itself. However, as time passed, these blessings were increasingly divorced from their liturgical context and were done privately by bishops and priests. With that separation from the Eucharistic celebration, the types and occasions for blessings proliferated. Kaczynski wrote, "The idea that there was magic at work inevitably grew

as soon as bishops and priests gave blessings privately, without any participation of the people."[12] Kaczynski added that these developments resulted
in a shifting emphasis from the praise of God and the community of the
faithful to an emphasis on the power of the priesthood to bless and on the
newly blessed object itself. Those responsible for rewriting Church blessings were thus mindful to ensure that people were present for the blessing
ritual and that blessings were accomplished within a liturgical structure. In
fact, the revised *Book of Blessings* stipulates, "The celebration of the blessing
of things or places according to custom should not take place without the
participation of at least some of the faithful."[13]

The drafters of the revised blessings clearly emphasized blessing people
over things. As noted previously, God's blessings apply preeminently to
people and through them to the rest of creation.[14] Thus, creation is thought
to be blessed when it is used in accord with God's creative plan to aid
human beings and in its proper role in salvation history. When objects are
blessed, the revised blessings will often note their function in God's saving
plan rather than simply blessing the objects in themselves.

For example, in the "Blessing of a Gymnasium" in the revised *Book of
Blessings*, the celebrant prays that the building will "contribute to leisure
activities that renew the spirit and strengthen mind and body" and that "all
who meet here may find the enrichment of companionship and together
offer you the praise."[15] The prayer is for the people and their welfare and
praising God, not for the building itself. As the General Introduction to the
book states, "Such blessings are invoked always with a view to the people
who use the objects to be blessed."[16]

Salesian priest and theologian Achille Triacca, who assisted the Congregation for the Sacraments and Divine Worship and later the Congregation for Divine Worship in the late 1970s, praised the new book. He
believed the change in emphasis was a "qualitative and quantitative jump"
forward,[17] and his review of the new book was ultimately positive.

When one reviews the revised *Book of Blessings*, these guiding principles for renewal are apparent. The blessings are structured as liturgical
celebrations requiring the presence of at least some of the faithful and a
scripture reading. They praise God and ask for his blessing on the people.
When objects are blessed, their role in aiding people and thus being part of
God's salvific plan is often explicitly included. Of these reforms, Kaczynski
wrote, "All this made it possible for the post-conciliar reform of blessings

to move beyond the narrow bounds of medieval practice and . . . to return
to the 'ancient and venerable norm of the Fathers.'"[18]

It is interesting and touching to hear of how Fr. Triacca died. Four days
before his death in October 2002, his old friend and collaborator Cardinal
Virgilio Noè, under whose signature the revised *De Benedictionibus* was
promulgated in 1984, visited him on his deathbed. Here is Cardinal Noè's
remembrance of those last moments:

> Those few minutes spent together, our hands clasped, were
> alternate moments of silence and dialogue. After a few fitting
> words Don Achille asked: "And at the office, how is it going?"
> At the end of the meeting I said: "My dear Don Achille you
> have always spoken and written about Liturgy here among us,
> now the time has come to move on, to the Liturgy of heaven.
> You have always spoken of the community of the faithful, now
> the time has come for you to join the community of the saints
> in the heavenly liturgy." He replied "give me your blessing." I
> placed my hands on his head and said the words of Blessing:
> May the Lord protect you, may He grant you his mercy and
> give you his peace.[19]

On his deathbed he asked for a priestly blessing. This blessing was imparted
by the cardinal laying his hands on his head and pronouncing the words
of blessing. Four days later, Fr. Triacca died.

RENEWAL OR DISTORTION?

The revised *Book of Blessings* received a mixed response. Some thought the
book was not a genuine renewal but actually a break with the tradition.
Dr. Daniel Van Slyke, comparing the blessing of holy water in the revised
and old rites, wrote, "The above analysis demonstrates that the present
Order is in no way derived from the previous Order; it is not a revision,
but an entirely new work."[20]

Some suggested that the revised blessings are not blessings at all. As
noted by Fr. Keith Kenney, "The critique often leveled against the 1984
De benedictionibus is that its prayers do not contain the words *bless, consecrate*, or *sanctify*, nor do they give expression to the apotropaic element
in blessings."[21] No doubt, as noted above, this was intentional. There
was clearly a movement away from directly blessing inanimate objects in

themselves. Rather, their role in aiding human beings and God's saving plan was emphasized. And there was the intention in the prayers to bless God and the people but not to exorcize any evil presence or influence.

Some theologians criticized the revision, citing its frequent lack of using such words as "bless," "consecrate," or "sanctify" in addition to the deletion of an apotropaic function.

One theologian, Alex Stock, described in the journal *Concilium* the changes in the blessing of baptismal water in the revised rite as a movement from actually blessing the water to a praising of God over the water. He spoke rather harshly of the changes and said they were a "disincarnation and dematerialization of the liturgical action of blessing."[22] By this he meant that the lack of blessing the object itself was a denial of the importance of the Incarnation and the sacramental nature of creation. In this view, priests should bless "things" as signs of the sacredness of all creation.

Moreover, Stock criticized the revised *De Benedictionibus* for "dematerializing" blessings. The point at hand is whether or not a blessing actually changes whatever is blessed in some real way. Does the blessed object itself carry a grace with it? Or does the use of the object become a grace only in that it aids the individual using it?

What is present here are two different worldviews and two different ways of conceiving how creation is blessed. For example, both the older and the revised blessings include a blessing of animals. As we see below, the older rite explicitly blesses the animals directly. The revised rite blesses the animals in their service to human beings, which is thought to be their proper use in the history of salvation. Both are called a blessing of animals, but they are based on different approaches. Let us look more closely at these two ways of blessing.

The Blessing of Animals

In the 1946 Weller version of the Roman Ritual, the "Blessing of Horses or Other Animals" calls for the priest to begin with the normal invocation:

> V. Our help is in the name of the Lord
> R. Who made heaven and earth.
> V. The Lord be with you.
> R. And with thy spirit.

Then there are three short prayers listed. The priest first asks God to "give ear to the entreaties of thy Church." He then prays for the people "to progress in virtue" by the example of St. Antony, who is associated in tradition with the blessing of animals. Finally, the priest sprinkles holy water on the animals and prays to God that they would "receive thy blessing," while making the Sign of the Cross, and prays that God may "deliver them from all harm."

Blessing of Horses or Other Animals (Weller, 1946)

Let these animals receive thy blessing, + O Lord,
to the benefit of their being,
and by the intercession of St. Antony, deliver them from all harm.
Through Christ our Lord. Amen.
They are sprinkled with holy water. [23]

Order for the Blessing of Animals (1989)

O God, the author and giver of every gift, animals also are part of the way you provide help for our needs and labors. We pray (through the intercession of Saint N.) that you will make available for our use the things we need to maintain a decent human life. We ask this through Christ our Lord. [24]

The 1989 revised *Book of Blessings* is quite different from the pre–Vatican II blessing of animals. The revised Order for the Blessing of Animals may be celebrated by a priest or a deacon; however, provision is also made for a layperson to lead the rite. After the opening Sign of the Cross and greeting, "the minister prepares those present for the blessing" through an instruction that puts the blessing in context. It is noted that "animals share in Christ's redemption of all of God's creation" and also that the Creator has set us over them. A selection from Genesis is read about God creating all creatures. A responsorial psalm is read with the people attending responding. God is directly praised: "O Lord, our God, how wonderful your name in all the earth!" Then, after a series of intercessions, the prayer of blessing is said. The priest or deacon with arms outstretched, or the layperson with folded hands, prays, "We pray that you will make available for our use the things we need to maintain a decent human life" or, in the second prayer option, "grant that these animals may serve our needs."[25] At the conclusion, the minister has the additional option of sprinkling the people and animals present.

One can readily see the differing theologies between the revised and old *De Benedictionibus*. The revised order is a richer liturgical event with a clear participation of the faithful. Moreover, one can see its praising of God and focus on the human person. On the other hand, the old rite is brief, requires a Sign of the Cross and holy water, and there is no provision for such blessings to be given by a layperson.

The old rite is clear that the animals themselves are intended to be blessed. The priest prays for the "benefit of their being" and to "deliver them from all harm."[26] The revised order, however, prays for human beings to be provided what is needed in life and to use animals rightly; the old blessing prays for the well-being of the animals themselves.

One can now readily see why some would ask if the revised order actually blesses the animals. But it is argued that the animals are blessed in the revised order through the blessing of the people present. In fact, the theology underlying the revised *Book of Blessings* was taken from Genesis, which is read during the ritual. In Genesis 1, God blesses man, made in his image, and commands him to have dominion over creation and to subdue it. In the intercessions, it is noted that God "created the animals and gave us the ability to train them to help us in our work."[27] The intercessions add that God's "lowliest creatures never cease to draw us toward your love."[28]

So as these creatures help human beings in their salvation journey, they fulfill their God-given role and are thought to be blessed.

However, this seemingly indirect way of blessing animals is not obvious in the order. It would be easy to be a bit disappointed in the revised order if one recalls the example of St. Francis and the centuries-old tradition of the blessing of animals in our churches. One might argue that a priest's blessing of the animals in themselves is part of our care for God's creation. These are two different approaches to what a blessing of creation means, which has contributed to misunderstandings.

But a nagging question remains: If animals themselves are blessed, what does it do for them? Or as the revised *Book of Blessings* seems to suggest: Does blessing animals directly in themselves foster superstition or magical thinking? We will take up this question again, later in this book.

THE BLESSING OF HOMES

One of the most widely requested blessings by priests is the blessing of homes. In previous days, it was routinely a part of the priest's duties and a regular part of the Church's ministry. Even in our secular age, it is still not uncommon for people to ask for their homes to be blessed.

Some of the first Latin blessings for a house are found in the eighth-century Gelasian Sacramentary. They pray for the blessing of the house and for its inhabitants.[29] In modern times, it was the custom in Rome for the priest to bless every house in his parish around Eastertime. The people would clean their houses *per il prete* and lay out their Easter meal on the table. He would bless the people, the food, and the home.

The reflection of a layperson who experienced the blessing of a home in Rome more than sixty years ago makes it clear that this pious woman believed that the blessing itself conferred a real grace on the home. She wrote: "Rooms that are spiritually refreshed and cleansed each year by this Paschal blessing are bound to be different from rooms that have never received it, and although often unaware of it, their inmates inhale an atmosphere of grace, fragrant and peaceful."[30] This woman believed that her blessed home was "refreshed and cleansed" and had an "atmosphere of grace, fragrant and peaceful." Is this a fanciful pious thought or a spiritual reality?

Let us now compare the old and revised rite for the blessing of homes. The old rite is very brief. The parish priest, accompanied by a server who carries the newly blessed Easter water, visits the homes of his parishioners on Holy Saturday or anytime during the Easter season. He sprinkles the homes and the people with the water, citing Ezekiel 47: "I saw water flowing from the right side of the temple." He then prays a very short prayer that includes asking a "holy angel from heaven to guard, cherish, protect, visit, and defend all who dwell in this house."[31]

A second prayer in the older rite for the blessing of homes outside of the Easter season was similar, although citing Psalm 51: "Sprinkle me with hyssop, O LORD, and I shall be clean: wash me, and I shall be whiter than snow."[32] A third option in the old rite, the blessing of homes during Epiphany, includes the Canticle of Mary from Luke 1 and the use of incense as well as holy water. While there are no explicit exorcistic elements in these blessings, the angels are asked to "guard" and "protect," which would likely be heard by those present as a protection from evil.[33]

The older rite is very brief, and one might say too brief if the family was hoping for a real celebration. There is no reading from scripture, and the overall brevity might be disappointing. However, if a priest was expected to bless every house in his parish, he could not be expected to do more in each location. No doubt, if time permitted, some priests using this older rite perhaps would add Bible readings and other prayers to add more solemnity and richness to the occasion.

ANOTHER BLESSING
OF A HOME (WELLER, 1946)

Thee, God the Father Almighty, we fervently implore for the sake of this home, and its occupants and possessions, that thou would bless + and sanctify + it, enriching it with every good. Pour out on them, O Lord, heavenly dew in good measure, as well as the fatness of earthly needs. Mercifully hear and grant the fulfillment of their prayers. And at our lowly coming, deign to bless + and sanctify + this home, as thou didst bless the homes of Abraham, Isaac, and

Jacob. Within these walls let thine angels of light preside and stand watch over them that dwell here. Through Christ our Lord. Amen. *It is sprinkled with holy water.* [34]

In the revised 1989 *Book of Blessings*, there is an order for the blessing of homes, and it is specifically for a "new home." The 1989 book also added an Order for the Blessing of Homes during the Christmas and Easter Seasons. The order does suggest that "when any of the faithful wish to mark their moving into a new home with a religious celebration, the parish priest . . . should gladly cooperate."[35]

ORDER FOR THE BLESSING OF A NEW HOME (1989)

Lord, be close to your servants who move into this home (today) and ask for your blessing. Be their shelter when they are at home, their companion when they are away, and their welcome guest when they return. And at last receive them into the dwelling place you have prepared for them in your Father's house, where you live for ever and ever. Amen. [36]

In the revised rite, after the initial greeting, there is a short instruction and a reading from scripture, with several options. A responsorial psalm follows, and then intercessions with responses from the faithful. Finally, there is a prayer of blessing, which petitions God to bless the people. Water is sprinkled on the new home, and the people "call to mind our baptism into Christ."[37] However, there is no Sign of the Cross explicitly indicated, whereas there are several in the old ritual.

It is interesting to read in the Introduction to the new order, "There is to be no blessing of a new home unless those who will live in it are present."[38] Certainly any priest can recognize the importance of having the family present during the home blessing for a variety of pastoral reasons. But the emphatic nature of the sentence implies that the presence of the people is necessary for such a blessing to be conferred.

It raises the question: If no one else is present and the priest blesses the home, is it blessed? But if the underlying theology is that blessings are not for objects or animals but for people, then the requirement that other people be present makes perfect sense. In the latter case, the blessing is then meant for the people and not the object itself.

In the revised blessing, once again we see a richer liturgical setting and a more inclusive participation of the faithful. However, there is no mention of actually blessing the home and certainly not of exorcizing it. Even the old rite only explicitly mentions blessing the home itself in "Another Blessing of a Home." In this blessing, the Sign of the Cross is made four times. At these four moments, the priest prays to "bless" and "sanctify" the home.[39] So the differences between the old and revised rites of blessings are not absolute: even in the pre–Vatican II house blessing, some of the prayers do not actually mention blessing the house itself.

Given that the *Book of Blessings* contains sacramentals and not sacraments, there is some leeway with the words of the prayers. In fact, ministers of these blessings are encouraged to adapt the words to fit the situation while maintaining the structure and major parts intact. Thus, if the home is not new, one might use the Order for the Blessing of a New Home and adjust the prayers as appropriate.

In today's parishes, it would be hard to envision a pastor of a large parish blessing every home on Holy Saturday, or even yearly. In my first parish of 1,200 families, it would have been impossible. However, I could envision a pastor blessing some homes of parishioners each year. Not only would it be a real grace imparted to the house and family but it could also be the occasion of a pastoral visit and connection of pastor to people.

With the reduced numbers of people who come to our churches on Sunday, this might be one way to reach out to those who have slipped away. Could families be contacted and asked if they would like the priest or deacon to come and bless their home and family? This might be especially timely if the family has just moved into the house and are now within the parish boundaries. No doubt, some lapsed Catholics would refuse the offer. But I suspect others would be grateful. Perhaps they might reconnect with the Church on this occasion. Likely God would give a special grace in that moment to any family that kindly opened its door to a priest or deacon.

In our increasingly secular age, the blessing of homes might be a good way for pastors to reach out to nonpracticing Catholics. The parish could offer that a priest or deacon visit and bless their homes. Blessings might be one way to connect with and serve those who do not come to church.

BLESSINGS AND THE NEW EVANGELIZATION

The differences between the old and revised blessings are striking. But, as noted, the differences are not absolute; there are areas of overlap. The clear differences do raise the importance of rediscovering the nature and power of the Church's blessings. Understanding and forming our priests in a proper understanding of the Church's blessings is likely more important today than ever.

In this secular age, as fewer step into our churches to receive the sacraments, it is important that we bring "church" to them. While they may not yet be receiving the full sacraments, anyone can receive a blessing. Canon 1170 states that blessings can be given "even to non-Catholics unless there is a prohibition of the Church to the contrary."[40] One need not check to make sure someone is in good standing as a practicing Catholic to lay one's hands on a person's head and pray.

I have blessed a number of nonpracticing Catholics and others of different faiths in a variety of places—stores, streets, airports, homes, and more. In each case, I had a sense that God had blessed those people through me. I suspected that some of them would never step foot into a Catholic church. However, I believe God touched them at that moment with a special grace. Perhaps this is central to the New Evangelization: bringing church to the people where they are.

It is rightly noted that sacramentals do not impart sanctifying grace as do the sacraments (*CCC* 1670). They do not bring one into a habitual state of grace, but the individual can receive graced spiritual effects. When a priest lays his hands on a person in blessing, in response to their willingness to receive such a blessing, certainly one can see the hand of God at work. If perhaps we have underestimated the power of the priestly blessing, it is likely that we have underestimated the power of God to work in the daily moments of our lives. And we may also be underestimating the full authority given to the Church by Jesus.

6.

HOLY WATER

Cleanse me with hyssop, that I may be pure;
wash me, and I will be whiter than snow.

—Psalm 51:9

BLESSING THE WATER

In pagan cultures water was thought to have a purifying and cleansing effect. In mythology, it was also believed to have supernatural powers.[1] Water, transformed by its Christian context, is used in the sacrament of Baptism. Through immersion or the pouring of the water, and the words of Baptism, the individual receives this first sacrament of Initiation and the beginning of the supernatural life of Christ.

Very early there emerged an actual blessing of the water itself before it was used in the sacrament. For example, in the fourth-century *Apostolic Constitutions*, we read about the water to be used for Baptism itself being first blessed:

> Look down from heaven, and sanctify this water; and bestow grace and power, so that he who is to be baptized, according to the command of thy Christ, may be crucified with him, and may die with him, and may be buried with him, and may rise with him to the adoption which is in him, by being made dead indeed unto sin, but alive unto righteousness.[2]

The water itself was blessed before it was used. God was asked to "bestow grace and power" on it so that the one baptized may die and rise with Christ.

Later the Gelasian Sacramentary also included a blessing over water to be sprinkled in the home.[3] The water was blessed and exorcized. Salt was also blessed and exorcized and mingled with the water. This mixing of exorcized salt and water to give us "holy water" was "universal in the Middle Ages" but began early in Church history.[4]

Water was also blessed at the Paschal Vigil for Baptism. The Gelasian Sacramentary blessing of baptismal water at the Paschal Vigil recalls God's work in creation and cleansing of the world through water. It asks God to increase his Church through the font of Baptism and to rebirth God's people into a new creation. Finally, the priest prays that "every unclean spirit depart from here, and may all the evils of the devil's deceit be far away." The ritual for blessing of holy water at the Paschal Vigil remained relatively unchanged for 1,200 years until the Second Vatican Council.[5]

In AD 852 in Reims, France, the archbishop wrote in "Chapters Given to Priests" the following instructions:

> That on every Sunday each priest in his church before the solemnities of the Masses should make blessed water . . . out of which the people entering the church may be sprinkled, and they who shall have wished may take from it . . . and may sprinkle it through their homes and fields and vineyards, also over their livestock and over their fodder, as well as over both their foods and their drink.[6]

In the revised post–Vatican II Rite of Baptism, the celebrant reads a beautiful "Blessing and Invocation of God over Baptismal Water." The prayer recalls the powerful role of water in salvation history, such as in the great flood, the parting of the Red Sea and the waters of the Jordan, water flowing from Jesus' side on the Cross, and water used by the disciples to baptize. Then the celebrant prays that God the Father with the Son send the Holy Spirit upon the water of the font so that those "who are buried with Christ in the death of baptism rise also with him to newness of life."[7] This prayer is not simply a remembrance of past events. It is precisely in recalling how God has acted powerfully in the history of salvation that we now, as the People of God, pray to be part of this salvation history. Just as the water has been a powerful instrument of God's salvation in the past, we pray that it become so now for us.

However, the ancient tradition of the water itself being cleansed or exorcized itself is not included. But it should be noted that the water itself is blessed as the celebrant touches it with his right hand and prays for the Holy Spirit to descend upon it. This physical gesture might remind us of the laying on of hands in other blessings and thus of the power of physical touch for the transmission of grace.

In all of these types of blessings of water, the substance is blessed and becomes "holy." Water is blessed in related but different contexts and for different purposes, such as for the sprinkling at Mass, for the fonts at the church entrance, for people to take home, for baptisms, and for the Easter Vigil. The use of holy water, made through a liturgical blessing, has been around for more than 1,500 years and is widespread throughout the Church. The sanctified water is then not only used for Baptism and sprinkling the faithful at Mass but, as time passed, was also sprinkled over just about everything—anything the people wanted blessed.

OLDER VERSUS REVISED RITE

The question "What is holy water?" is an important one when discussing priestly blessings. Simply put, one might say that holy water is water that has been blessed by a priest. And so another question comes to the fore: What does it mean for a priest to bless the water? Does the water become different? Or should we focus rather on its function? In other words, what is water's function in God's salvific will for each of us in particular and for salvation history as a whole?

When we look at the older rite of blessing water and compare it to the revised *Book of Blessings*, we see a very different approach. In the older rite, such as in the Gelasian Sacramentary, first the salt is exorcized and blessed. Then the water is exorcized and blessed. The two are mixed together, and a final prayer is said. In the exorcism of the water, the priest prays the following prayer:

Blessing of
Holy Water (Weller, 1946)

Thou creature of water, I purge thee of evil in the name of God + the Father almighty, in the name of Jesus + Christ, His Son, our Lord, and in the power of the Holy + Spirit, that thou mayest be water fit to brace us against the envious foe. Mayest thou be empowered to drive him forth and exile him together with his fallen angels by the power of the selfsame Jesus Christ, our Lord Who shall come to judge the living and the dead, and the world by fire. Amen.[8]

This is very different from the revised Order for the Blessing of Holy Water outside Mass. Presumably, a priest or deacon should not do the blessing by himself, since the General Introduction says, "The celebration of the blessing of things or places according to custom should not take place without the participation of at least some of the faithful."[9]

Like the other blessings in the book, it is clearly a liturgical celebration with introductory words, a reading, and then the actual prayer of blessing:

Blessing of
Holy Water outside Mass (1989)

Blessed are you, Lord, all-powerful God, who in Christ, the living water of salvation, blessed and transformed us. Grant that, when we are sprinkled with this water or make use of it, we will be refreshed inwardly by the power of the Holy Spirit and continue to walk in the new life we received at baptism. We ask this through Christ our Lord. Amen.[10]

The old blessing of water emphasizes its exorcistic function and exorcized the water and salt first. The priest prayed, "I purge thee of evil," thus suggesting that the water itself needed first to be sanctified. In contrast, the revised blessing focuses on the human person. The blessing is designed so that we might be "refreshed inwardly." Particularly in its opening remarks, the revised blessing is meant to remind us of our Baptism.

It is striking how different these revised and older prayers are. The revised prayer does not contain an exorcistic function or even an apotropaic function, and the old contains no reference to the sacrament of Baptism.

The *Catechism* states that sacramentals are "sacred signs which bear a resemblance to the sacraments," and "by them men are disposed to receive the chief effect of the sacraments, and various occasions in life are rendered holy" (*CCC* 1667). It seems that the older rite, in focusing so heavily on the exorcistic function of holy water, did not encompass a broader vision including Baptism. In the Church's history, holy water emerged from the sacrament of Baptism and, if it is faithful to its identity, must first remain connected to this sacrament in all its effects.

On the other hand, the *Catechism* indicates that, through the use of sacramentals, occasions in life are "rendered holy." The revised rite is limited with regard to this sanctifying role. In what way does holy water itself sanctify an occasion? Moreover, there is a long history of the use of holy water to cleanse and cast out evil.

It is important to note that in Appendix II of the current *Roman Missal*, there is a "Rite for the Blessing and Sprinkling of Water," which has a more traditional wording for the blessing of holy water. It blesses the water itself and prays for "protection . . . against all illness and every snare of the enemy." Also, the rite includes the option of mixing the blessed salt and water, and the celebrant prays over the salt that the "impure water might be purified" and "every attack of the enemy repulsed."[11]

In Appendix II of the current *Roman Missal*, the blessing of water allows a mixing of blessed salt and water; it contains a positive reference to protection against evil, and it speaks of sanctification; and it remains connected to its baptismal roots. It is a good example of combining all these important elements of the tradition of blessing water.

――――――――――――――――――――――――――――――

So priests have this option in the Roman Ritual, which is more in line with pre–Vatican II blessings. And yet, like the revised order of blessing, its opening words make an important link to the sacrament of Baptism and set the context for the meaning of holy water: "Bless this water . . . as a memorial of our Baptism." The priest prays that we "remain faithful to the Spirit we have received" in this sacrament.[12]

Thus we see in this ritual a salutary confluence of the new and the old, a focusing on its connection to the sacraments without losing its role in purification and sanctification. The blessing recognizes the reality of evil without losing its focus on our new life of grace in Jesus. Could this not be the beginning of a model for further development in our understanding and practice of blessings?

THE EXORCISTIC FUNCTION OF HOLY WATER

The words of St. Teresa of Avila about holy water from her autobiography are instructive and deserve to be cited at length:

> From long experience I have learned that there is nothing like holy water to put devils to flight and prevent them from coming back again . . . so holy water must have great virtue. For my own part, whenever I take it, my soul feels a particular and most notable consolation. In fact, it is quite usual for me to be conscious of a refreshment which I cannot possibly describe, resembling an inward joy which comforts my whole soul. This is not fancy, or something which has happened to me only once: it has happened again and again and I have observed it most attentively. . . . It makes me very happy to find that those words of the Church are so powerful that they impart their power to the water and make it so very different from water which has not been blessed.[13]

It is just such anecdotes that continue to encourage an exorcistic function for holy water as well as supporting the traditional belief that there is something profoundly different about holy water from regular water. St. Teresa, a Doctor of the Church, suggests that there is a real grace attached to using holy water.

St. Teresa said that holy water "put[s] devils to flight" and also gave her a "most notable consolation." Its use by the faithful for protection from evil and sanctification ought to be promoted, and it should be made readily available to take home.

Holy water holds a central role in both the old and revised rites of exorcism. One of the main signs of a demonic presence is an aversion to holy things, such as the relics of saints, a crucifix, and holy water. A common practice among exorcists to assist in discerning a demonic presence, as well as in ultimately casting it out, is to sprinkle holy water on the individual.

There is a long history of holy water being used as an exorcistic element. This will not disappear. The exorcistic function of holy water arose fairly early in the Church and continues unabated to our day. The experience of saints such as Teresa of Avila and the practice of exorcists is rooted in deep spiritual realities, and the pious use of holy water in protecting people from evil is not to be discouraged but rather ought to be promoted in the proper context of faith.

Holy water importantly reminds us of our Baptism. The faithful should be encouraged to take it home and to use it often to strengthen their baptismal faith as well as for its functions of cleansing and protecting from evil.

However, if the exorcistic function becomes dominant in our understanding of holy water, or any sacramental, it indeed lends itself to superstitious practices. When sacramentals are divorced from the sacraments and are separated from their true faith context, then they easily become talismans harkening back to a pre-Judeo-Christian era. As we recall, it is the witness of scripture that all blessings ultimately come from God and thus only make sense within a proper context of faith.

Moreover, it is dangerous to fall into a kind of obsession or fascination with evil. The modern proliferation of movies and television stories about evil with the concomitant decline of faith in society makes one wonder if our obsession with evil and the demonic is itself not a subtle ploy of Satan. Those of us who profess faith in Jesus should look to God and to the heavens, and not cast our gaze downward toward the infernal regions.

Jesus sent out the disciples two by two to cure the sick and proclaim the kingdom (see Lk 10:1), and he "gave them authority over unclean spirits" (Mk 6:7). The disciples returned exultant and said, "Lord, even the demons are subject to us because of your name." Jesus affirmed their insight, "I have observed Satan fall like lightning from the sky," but then he added, "Nevertheless, do not rejoice because the spirits are subject to you, but rejoice because your names are written in heaven" (Lk 10:17–18, 20). Our great joy is our communion with God and the saints. While we should not dismiss the exorcistic ministry, our eyes as Christians must remain focused on Jesus and the light, not on the darkness.

As St. Teresa mentioned, while holy water casts out the demons, it also gave her a conscious refreshment that was a comfort to her soul. In our use of holy water, we ought to be reminded of our Baptism. It ought to remind us that we are children of God. We pray that as we too use holy water, we might receive a grace to live out our Baptism with greater integrity. And perhaps God might also grant us, like St. Teresa, a consoling grace to remind us of his abiding presence and love.

Blessing Expectant Mothers

Holy water was also used, at times, in healing pregnant women with troubled pregnancies. Theodoret of Cyrus, bishop and theologian, in fifth-century Syria told of how his mother had a difficult pregnancy and he, as her child in utero, was in danger of death. His mother asked the famous hermit Macedonius to help her. He blessed some water and said to her, "Drink this water, and you shall perceive the divine remedy."[14] A similar story is recounted of the abbot St. Bernard of Clairvaux blessing holy water and giving it to a woman suffering a difficult pregnancy. She too gave birth safely.[15]

Such stories reflect not only the long-standing belief that God blesses people through the use of holy water but also the long tradition of holy women and men who are not clerics being able to bless. The faithful have long recognized the power of saintly people to convey special blessings—in this case, Macedonius the hermit. These stories also demonstrate the use of holy water as an instrument to convey such blessings.

There is an established history of blessing children in utero and their mothers. With the dangers of childbirth and the Church's consistent belief in the sacredness of the unborn child's life, it was natural that the Church would provide a blessing for pregnant women as one of its early liturgical blessings.[16]

In the tenth century in a ritual from Mainz, Germany, a blessing for a woman in labor is provided:

> O God, who from the beginning made man and gave him a helpmate similar to himself, that they should increase and multiply upon the earth, grant your mercy to this your maidservant [Name], that she may bring forth favorably and without sorrow.[17]

This tradition of blessing pregnant women continues to our day. The revised *Book of Blessings* contains both a long and short form of "Blessing Parents before Childbirth." This liturgical blessing includes prayers, a reading from scripture, a psalm, a litany, and the Our Father with a final blessing:

> Gracious Father, your Word, spoken in love, created the human family and, in the fullness of time, your Son, conceived in love, restored it to your friendship. Hear the prayers of N. and N., who await the birth of their child. Calm their fears when they are anxious. Watch over and support these parents and bring their child into this world safely and in good health, so that as members of your family they may praise you and glorify you through your Son, our Lord Jesus Christ, now and for ever. Amen.[18]

The priest or deacon with arms outstretched then pronounces the final blessing with the Sign of the Cross: "And may almighty God bless you all, the Father, and the Son, + and the Holy Spirit."[19] This blessing may also be celebrated by a lay minister or family member; however, the prayer of blessing is then said with hands folded. There is no mention of holy water in either case.

This blessing may be celebrated anytime during the pregnancy. The *Book of Blessings* also provides for a blessing immediately before childbirth and also after childbirth for the mother if she is unable to attend the Baptism.

While priests offering a blessing should approach the situation with sensitivity, blessings for expectant parents ought to be offered regularly. The courage and generosity of the parents in bringing new life into the world ought to be affirmed and supported.

Because of the advances in medical science, maternal and infant mortality in childbirth has declined markedly. But the rate is not zero, and for most parents, pregnancy and birthing remain a source of expectant joy but also a cause of anxiety. The pregnant women I have seen receive a priestly blessing were very grateful.

While approaching such a situation with sensitivity, should our pastors and shepherds not be offering the Church's blessing to expectant parents on a regular basis? Their courage in bringing their child to birth participates most directly in God's earliest charge to humankind: "Be fertile and multiply" (Gn 1:28). No doubt God would want us to be generous in sharing his blessings with these courageous parents and their vulnerable children.

7.

WHO CAN BLESS?

Whoever believes in me will do the works that I do, and will do greater ones than these.

—John 14:12

EMPOWERING LAY MINISTRY

At the Second Vatican Council, the issue of who can bless was debated. There was a movement toward limiting blessings to priests and bishops. Some argued that allowing the laity to bless would change the nature of sacramentals.

However, it was pointed out that the history of the Church includes laypeople giving blessings in certain circumstances. Notably, the third-century *Apostolic Tradition* is very clear that either a cleric or a layperson can bless catechumens preparing for Baptism:

> At the close of their prayer, when their instructor lays his hand upon the catechumens, he shall pray and dismiss them; whoever gives the instruction is to do this, whether a cleric or a layman.[1]

Other convincing arguments were made, including the necessity of lay catechists and other lay pastoral leaders in missionary lands blessing the people in the absence of clerics. There are many such areas where priests visit only rarely. For example, in some African nations, lay catechists functionally lead the community and teach the faith. It only makes sense that they would be empowered by the Church to bless the people.

As noted previously, there is a long tradition of holy people blessing and being earnestly sought out by the pious for their blessing. One particularly interesting anecdote is the effectiveness of St. Catherine of Siena in casting out demons. It was said that if the priests were not able to exorcize a possessed person, they would send the person to St. Catherine, whose blessing would immediately cast out the demons.[2] The Church only allows priests to conduct major or solemn exorcisms in its name—that is, formally casting out demons from a possessed person—with the permission of the local bishop (*CCC* 1673). However, the ability of a holy person or a layperson with a particular charism to expel demons has long been recognized. The Church appoints priests to bless, but the blessing of the saint often proves most powerful.

The proposal that suitable laity could be empowered to bless in certain circumstances was passed at the Second Vatican Council. *Sacrosanctum Concilium* thus states, "Let provision be made that some sacramentals, at least in special circumstances and at the discretion of the ordinary, may be administered by qualified lay persons" (*SC* 79). This is echoed in the *Catechism of the Catholic Church*: "Sacramentals derive from the baptismal priesthood: every baptized person is called to be a 'blessing,' and to bless. Hence lay people may preside at certain blessings." But then the *Catechism* adds, "The more a blessing concerns ecclesial and sacramental life, the more is its administration reserved to the ordained ministry (bishops, priests, or deacons)" (*CCC* 1669).

So it is firmly part of the Church's magisterium that the laity can bless in some circumstances and at the discretion of the ordinary. Certainly, though, the Judeo-Christian tradition rather early focused the role of blessings on the priesthood. From the blessings of Aaron to today, it is recognized that priestly ordination carries with it the power to bless in the name of the Church.

The laity, because of their Baptism, can bless "in special circumstances and at the discretion of the ordinary." They ought to be encouraged to bless. The *Book of Blessings* indicates a number of instances for them to exercise their priesthood of the faithful.

Canon 1168 suggests that blessings reside primarily with clerics because of the sacred power conferred in ordination. It states, "The minister of sacramentals is a cleric who has been provided with the requisite power." So it seems that blessings are typically the reserve of clerics. However, it should be added that priests and deacons only bless under the authority of the local bishop.[3] Canon 1168 further recognizes that laity "can also administer some sacramentals" based upon the "judgment of the local ordinary" and "according to the norm of the liturgical books."[4] So one might say that the Code of Canon Law envisions that clerics would be the ones to give blessings except in some circumstances that are specified wherein laity can bless.

But this focus on the requisite power of clerics for blessing ought not to disempower the priesthood of the faithful, which would, in fact, be a form of clericalism. Pope Francis has repeatedly warned the Church about the dangers of clericalism, which he sees very much alive in today's Church. An important reform of the Second Vatican Council was a recognition of the priesthood of the faithful and, in this case, its role in blessings.

The *Catechism*'s statement that all the baptized can bless reminds me of a regular encounter I have with a female usher at the ballpark where I am a chaplain. I often go by her post, and she regularly asks me for a blessing. She is not Catholic but rather a strong evangelical Christian whose faith I find inspiring. She is very appreciative when this priestly blessing is given to her. After I lay my hands on her head and bless her, she will then give me a blessing in return. I willingly bow my head and receive her blessing. There is no doubt in my mind that God is blessing me at that moment through her intercession.

LAITY IN THE *BOOK OF BLESSINGS*

The General Introduction of the revised *Book of Blessings* does not speak of giving blessings based upon inherent powers but rather "in keeping with the place and office within the people of God belonging to each person." Thus, bishops are to preside when the blessings involve the entire diocesan community. When the parish community gathers, the priest who is appointed to preside over that community should be the one to preside over the blessings. Deacons assist the bishop and the priests and preside in their absence. Acolytes and readers, who have been formally installed as such (typically ministries on the path to ordination in the United States), may preside over specified blessings, as may the laity in general, particularly exercising their role as parents.[5] The General Introduction stipulates, "But whenever a priest or a deacon is present, the office of presiding should be left to him."[6]

The revised *Book of Blessings* gives many opportunities for the laity to preside. For example, they can bless travelers, ecumenical groups, students and teachers, catechumens, the sick, the elderly, parents before childbirth, and children. The blessing of religious articles and rosaries, however, requires a priest or deacon. Laity can bless new homes, animals, fields, and flocks. In the home, the laity may bless an Advent wreath, a nativity scene, and a Christmas tree.

Clearly, the revised *Book of Blessings* based the authority to bless on the baptismal priesthood, as indicated by the *Catechism of the Catholic Church*. But there is a hierarchy implicit in the blessings. While there is a wide scope for the laity to bless, if a priest or deacon is present, he should preside.

HANDS FOLDED OR ARMS OUTSTRETCHED

There is an interesting difference in many of the blessings. If a priest or deacon is present, he is instructed to say the prayer of blessing "with hands outstretched," whereas the "lay minister says the prayer with hands joined." This is repeated over and over again, from blessing to blessing. Perhaps it is just a customary practice: the priest or deacon typically prays at the altar with arms outstretched, whereas the laity prays with hands folded. Or it may be an indication of a difference in roles.

The arms outstretched, or *orans* position, is a sign of the person praying, but in liturgical services it represents the priest or deacon praying on behalf of the people assembled. He stands as the leader of the assembly, and he gives voice to the prayer of the entire community. While the lay presider of a blessing is actually leading the assembly, he or she still prays with hands folded. Why?

As one looks at the *Book of Blessings* itself and also at the long history of the sign of priestly blessings, the priest not only outstretches his hands in the *orans* position while praying but also will typically stretch his arms over the individual or thing he is blessing. He may even lay his hands on the individual or object in the act of blessing. He typically does this while reciting the prayer of blessing.

This posture is reflected in the revised *Book of Blessings*. For the blessing of the sick, the priest or deacon in the first prayer option is instructed to "lay his hands on the head of each sick person" and recite the prayer of blessing. The lay minister may only "trace the sign of the cross on the forehead of each sick person" in reciting the prayer.[7] Similarly, in the Order for the Blessing of a Family, "the priest or deacon says the prayer of blessing with hands outstretched over the family members" while the lay minister "says the prayer with hands joined."[8]

Even in the blessing of children, in which parents have a special authority (Order for the Blessing of Sons and Daughters), the parents "trace the sign of the cross on their children's forehead." In the Orders for the Blessing of Children, however, the priest or deacon prays with "hands outstretched over the children" or "laying his hands on the child."[9]

As I read this, I notice that there is an implication that this act of stretching out one's hands in blessing is a sign of the ordained cleric. Is there also an implication that God's grace is moving through the instrument of the priest, especially his hands? It seems to be so. Similarly, in the ordination of the priest, it is a critical part of the Rite of Ordination for the presiding bishop to lay his hands on the head of the ordinand. The sign suggests that the grace of ordination coming from God flows through the bishop directly to the priest.

Time and again we witness this essentially priestly gesture of stretching out his hands over the people in blessing. At the end of the Mass, when a solemn blessing is given, the priest is instructed to stretch out his hands over the people and pronounce the blessing.

If laypeople were to stretch out their hands in these blessings or lay on hands in blessing, no doubt it would look odd to some Catholics. One might argue that it is just that they are not accustomed to seeing the laity use such a gesture. But it seems that the gesture belongs to the ordained cleric. This notion is implicitly recognized in the revised *Book of Blessings*.

INVOKING VERSUS IMPARTING A BLESSING

The sign of the laying on of hands or stretching out of the priest's hands over the person or object in blessings suggests to this author that the priest is *imparting* a blessing. He is not only invoking a blessing from God but also there is a power given to him to impart a blessing to others. The fact that there is a "sacred power" to the priesthood was recognized by the Second Vatican Council (*LG* 10) and the *Catechism of the Catholic Church*: "The ministerial priesthood differs in essence from the common priesthood of the faithful because it confers a sacred power" (*CCC* 1592). But both *Lumen Gentium* and the *Catechism* note that this sacred power is to be used in service to the faithful.

A somewhat amusing and inspiring story of a bishop's "blessing" comes from the biography of the saintly archbishop of Canterbury, Bl. Lanfranc of Pavia (d. ca. 1089). He died and was laid out on a bier in the cathedral.[10] "A pious old woman hobbled in through the screen, took his hand, and blessed herself. His relics healed her of a two-year paralysis of her feet."[11] This story reminds us that the sacramentals grow out of the pious devotion of the faithful and respond to their needs. Moreover, one suspects that both the faith of this woman and the intercession of the archbishop were instrumental in this miraculous cure. It seems that the archbishop truly "blessed" her.

Of course, this power comes from God and is only effective with God's dynamic presence, much as the Old Testament prophets' words were powerful only because it was God who inspired them. While the revised *Book of Blessings* does not address the issues of powers directly, the long history of the Church suggests that there is a unique power of blessing in the ordained priesthood. Some might argue that this is a form of clericalism or belongs to a bygone era. But the notion remains strongly rooted in our tradition.

Priests impart blessings through the "sacred power" entrusted to them from God. A priest is an instrument of God's blessings. This power is used in service to "sanctify the Christian people and offer sacrifice to God."

In the pre–Vatican II Rite of Ordination, the priest's hands were anointed with the oil of catechumens, and the bishop announced, "What they bless shall be blessed, and what they consecrate shall be consecrated and sanctified, in the name of Jesus Christ our Lord."[12] In explaining this text, Dom Pierre de Puniet wrote, "He blesses by virtue of his ordination and of the sacred character with which his ordination has invested him."[13]

In the revised post–Vatican II rite, the ordinand's hands are anointed with holy chrism, and the bishop prays, "The Lord Jesus Christ, whom the Father anointed with the Holy Spirit and power, guard and preserve you that you may sanctify the Christian people and offer sacrifice to God."[14]

The revised rite speaks of sanctifying the people in general, which is a broad mandate, while the older rite spoke of the power to bless, consecrate, and sanctify. While the revised rite does not specifically mention this power to bless, one naturally presumes that it is not absent in those ordained using the revised Rite of Ordination. Rather, the rite emphasizes different aspects of priestly ordination, but the ordination that men received in both the old and revised rites is the same. The essence of the priesthood has not changed, even as its mode of expression must vary with the time and culture.

This direct imparting of a grace is second nature to a priest. In the confessional using the Roman Rite, he says in the first person to the penitent, "I absolve you from your sins." Priests recognize that it is only God's power that can absolve sins, but God gives this power to priests in the sacrament of Holy Orders. The words of scripture are applied directly to the priest: "Whose sins you forgive are forgiven them, and whose sins you retain are retained" (Jn 20:23). Similarly, the priest prays the words of Christ himself during the consecration at the Mass: "This is my body. . . . This is my blood." The priest prays those words in the first person, acting in the person of Christ. He is not simply recalling a historical event but is making present the Eucharistic Christ through his priesthood.

The reality of the priest acting in the person of Christ is a daunting reality when faced head on. It would be easy to shy away from it and downplay it. But this would be to betray the reality of the Catholic priesthood. Rather than leading us to clericalism, it should be a source of humility for priests. Instead of causing us to reverence the priesthood, it ought to make us reverence God, who has given such grace to the Church. Jesus promised his disciples, "Whoever believes in me will do the works that I do, and will do greater ones than these" (Jn 14:12). Just as Jesus blessed the children and also gave his final blessing to his disciples when he was taken up into heaven (see Lk 24:51), so do priests continue his ministry of blessing and sanctifying.

Such graces are necessary if the fullness of the mandate given to priests is to be realized. In the revised rite for ordination, the priest is "ordained for the sanctification of the Christian people." The priestly blessing, in all its forms, is an important part of that function. Through the blessings of the Church, the priest helps to sanctify the people in their everyday lives and the world we all inhabit. The sacraments are typically great moments of grace in the exceptional experiences of life (along with the salutary practicing of daily Eucharist and frequent confession). Blessings are not only part of these sacraments but also can, and should, be part of the everyday lives of the people.

The use of blessings, and sacramentals in general, is a way to sanctify the ordinary moments in one's life. In this era of secularization, these can be especially important in strengthening one's daily life of faith. Blessings ought to be widely promoted.

If people are not using holy water fonts in their houses, blessing their homes and their children, blessing their fields and workplaces, blessing their meals and their travel, are they not missing something? Perhaps it is just another sign of the creeping secularism in our time. If we relegate God and the Church to one hour on Sunday (if that!), and perhaps a few peak moments in our lives, we cannot be said to be living a fully Christian life. All of life is meant to be sacred and filled with God's presence and his blessings. The kingdom of God is around us and in us in every place and in every moment of our lives. Blessings and sacramentals are one way to remind us of that and to welcome a conscious, actual grace in our daily lives. Without them, our lives are spiritually poorer.

Deacons Blessing

Deacons are featured prominently in the revised *Book of Blessings*. It is clear that they are commissioned by the Church to bless. There has been some question as to the status of deacons regarding blessings. But deacons are ordained clerics, and thus it is proper to include them in any discussion of the ordained clergy.

For example, in the revised *Book of Blessings*, the Order for the Blessing of Religious Articles may be prayed by a priest or a deacon. These objects include such items as medals, small crucifixes, statues, and rosaries. There is no provision in this order for the laity to bless religious objects. Similarly, there is a separate Order for the Blessing of Rosaries, and again only priests and deacons are mentioned as those who may preside.[15]

Deacons, as ordained clerics, have an important place in the revised *Book of Blessings* and may bless people and religious objects.

A deacon may also preside over any of those blessings that may be presided over by the laity. If a deacon or a priest is present, then he should preside. If both a deacon and priest are present, then the priest should preside with the deacon assisting by "carrying out those functions proper to the diaconate."[16] The revised ritual recognizes this ecclesial hierarchy.

It is interesting that the Order for the Blessing of Holy Water outside Mass also reserves the authority to priests and deacons and not the laity. Among the sacramentals, there is something special about holy water, as noted previously in this text. From the earliest centuries of Christianity until today, holy water has been valued by the clergy and the laity. Moreover, holy water is related to the "ecclesial and sacramental life" of the Church, so its blessing is properly reserved to the ordained clergy (*CCC* 1669).

In 2009, Pope Benedict XVI issued a *motu proprio, Omnium in Mentem,* which added a third paragraph to Canon 1009: "Those who are constituted in the order of the episcopate or the presbyterate receive the mission and capacity to act in the person of Christ the Head, whereas deacons are empowered to serve the People of God in the ministries of the liturgy, the Word, and charity." Deacons are empowered to bless, but this *motu proprio* makes it clear that the blessing does not come from someone acting *in persona Christi capitis*.[17] This suggests that deacons invoke rather than impart blessings, unlike priests.

Only priests, and not deacons, may administer the sacrament of the Anointing of the Sick. The Holy See has been clear about this.[18] The sacrament contains an absolution from sin, and only a priest or bishop acting *in persona Christi capitis* can forgive sins.

Nevertheless, the revised *Book of Blessings* contains Orders for the Blessing of the Sick, which are not sacraments but rather *sacramentals*. Happily, deacons and laity may preside over such blessings.[19] In this ritual, the priest or deacon may "lay his hands on the head of each sick person, and then say the prayer of blessing."[20] The lay minister traces the Sign of the Cross on their foreheads.

Only a priest or bishop may administer the sacrament of the Anointing of the Sick; however, deacons and laity can give formal blessings. They ought to be encouraged to give these blessings when visiting the sick.

Only a priest or deacon may use the short formulary: "May he who alone is Lord and Redeemer bless + you, N. May he give health to your body and holiness to your soul. May he bring you safely to eternal life. Amen."[21]

While this blessing of the sick is not a sacrament, it is a sacramental, and it offers God's blessings to the sick. By extending the remit to use this order to the diaconate and the laity, the Church generously makes this blessing now more widely available. Should it not be used with more frequency? There are many, many sick people who would be grateful and profit from such a blessing.

Baptismal and Ordained Priesthood in Harmony

Both the laity and the clergy can bless because they are baptized, as noted in the *Catechism*. But some situations require a priest or deacon to bless, as clearly provided for in the revised *Book of Blessings*. There are also times when it would be most appropriate for the laity to bless. For example, when a child celebrates a birthday or goes off to college or at some other important event, a parent's blessing is irreplaceable.

In these moments, the layperson prays with hands folded and *invokes* (rather than *imparts*) a blessing over the child. The parent prays asking God to bless his or her child. Parents *invoke* blessings in their roles as baptized Christians and with the God-given authority of parents. When a priest prays, however, due to the character of Holy Orders, he *imparts* a blessing. The priest is acting both *in persona ecclesiae* and *in persona Christi capitis*.[22]

It should be noted that there are theologians who disagree. They would say that blessings are given by the authority of the Church and do not have any connection with the grace of priestly ordination. Thus, the blessing by the lay minister and the priest would be received from God in the same mode. But the long history of the Church and of pastoral practice, as noted, suggests otherwise.

If the Church started having the laity use similar gestures as priests with their hands, it would seem to many that something is amiss. It could be seen as a kind of clericalizing of the laity and thus a subtle downplaying of the importance of their own true vocation. The laity are not priests with limited powers. The baptismal priesthood and the ordained priesthood are not different in degree but different in essence (*LG* 10; *CCC* 1592). One is not better than the other, but they are different and have different functions. Still, both priests and laity participate in the one priesthood of Christ and ought to embrace fully their unique role in that priesthood.

The blessings of the baptismal priesthood and the ordained priesthood are different in essence, not degree. The laity should be encouraged to bless, especially in those situations where they are uniquely important, such as a parent blessing a child when a child becomes engaged or goes off to school, or a lay catechist blessing the catechumens.

It is a useless speculation to ask whether one blessing is more effective than the other. There is always a danger of excessively reifying grace. Grace has already been made concrete in Jesus Christ and thus reified in some way. The supernatural has become human and entered our created world. Thus grace is a real, dynamic force in our world. But to try to quantify grace as being *more* or *less* in one particular situation over against another is ill-advised and potentionally misleading.

Moreover, the efficacy of a blessing likely depends upon many factors. One could easily see how the blessing of a parent over an engaged son or daughter would seem more appropriate and perhaps more effective than any grace a priest might offer at that point. But the revised *Book of Blessings* maintains a hierarchical structure, and if a priest or deacon is present, he is typically the one to preside.

The Second Vatican Council suggested that a corrective was needed. The power of the ordained priesthood to bless was previously well recognized. However, the authority of the baptismal priesthood to bless was not. Thus, it called for clearer recognition of the baptismal priesthood and its proper role in sacramentals. This was largely obscured before the Council, as was the overall role of the laity in bringing about the kingdom.

Would not our children today be richly blessed if their baptized parents recognized their God-given authority to bless them and exercised it? Do catechumens not receive a wonderful blessing when the catechist who instructs them presides over their blessing? When a young couple becomes engaged, it is most fitting, as recognized in the revised *Book of Blessings*, that one of the parents presides over their blessing.[23] And in missionary lands, especially in the absence of clerics, the lay leaders and catechists of parishes appropriately invoke God's blessings on their people.

There is much work for us priests and deacons in reviving these important blessings presided over by the laity. While not confusing the blessing of the ordained priesthood with the baptismal priesthood, the proper and important role of the laity in these sacramentals needs to be encouraged. The grace of the ordained priesthood and the baptismal priesthood ought to work in harmony. The work of the parents and the priest with young people, for instance, complement each other. Each priesthood has its own role and function, neither one more important than the other but each an integral part of God's plan. And both are an expression of the one priesthood of Jesus Christ.

8.

THE NATURE
OF BLESSINGS:
DISPUTED QUESTIONS

Into whatever house you enter, first say, "Peace to this
household." If a peaceful person lives there, your peace
will rest on him; but if not, it will return to you.

—Luke 10:5–6

ACTUAL GRACED EFFECTS

As the Church has developed its understanding of sacramentals down
through the centuries and also distinguished them from the Seven Sacraments, it defined a blessing as a sacramental. However, as noted in the
Catechism, "among sacramentals blessings (of persons, meals, objects, and
places) come first" (*CCC* 1671). While I would not suggest making blessings an eighth sacrament, the *Catechism* itself points to their importance.
Also, the former Rite of Ordination of a priest indicated the importance
of blessings in the priestly ministry and thus for the life of the Church:
"What they bless shall be blessed."[1]

Nevertheless, the blessing does not directly bring with it sanctifying
grace. St. Thomas Aquinas did say that a blessing or asperges with holy
water can be the occasion of a remission of venial sin: "This [venial sin]

is taken away by certain sacramentals, for instance, Holy Water and such like" (*ST* III, q. 65, art. 1, ad 8).[2] He pointed out the importance of such actions and stirring up in those receiving the blessing the fervor of charity as an important aspect of the blessing's efficacy.[3]

The grace of a blessing, as a sacramental, points to the central graces of the sacraments and assists one in living out those foundational graces.[4] Canon 1166 states, "Sacramentals are sacred signs by which effects, especially spiritual effects, are signified in some imitation of the sacraments and are obtained through the intercession of the Church."[5] In the case of a blessing with holy water, not only is the person blessed reminded of his or her Baptism but the Catholic faith would also posit that an actual graced "effect" is offered through the intercession of the Church. This effect helps individuals in living out their lives as adopted sons and daughters of God.

GRACE OFFERED

Is a grace always received when a blessing is given? *Sacraments* confer grace *ex opere operato*, by virtue of the rite itself. We should remind ourselves that this is, of course, not magic. The rite of a sacrament confers the grace because the sacraments have been instituted by Jesus himself; and so ultimately they are the gift of God. On the other hand, whether a graced effect is received from sacramentals depends also upon the disposition of the recipient; that is, *ex opere operantis*.[6] A sacramental's grace also presumes the intercession of the Church for its efficacy and, ultimately of course, the mercy of God (*CCC* 1667, 1670).

The Gospel of Luke is instructive in this regard. Jesus sent his disciples out two by two and instructed them, "Into whatever house you enter, first say, 'Peace to this household.' If a peaceful person lives there, your peace will rest on him; but if not, it will return to you" (Lk 10:5–6). This greeting, "Peace to this household," is an ancient greeting and blessing used in first encountering another, as previously discussed in this book's chapter on the Old Testament. Jesus is clear that the blessing is only conferred "if a peaceful person lives there." Otherwise, the blessing returns to the one who offered it.

Thus, the grace of a blessing may be offered but not always received. When a priest blesses, as the old Rite of Ordination indicated, the blessing is transmitted. This is reminiscent of God's promise to Aaron, as previously cited: "This is how you shall bless the Israelites. . . . And I will bless them" (Nm 6:23, 27). However, the blessing may not be received if the person is not willing. So before I bless someone, I typically ask, "Would you like me to give you a blessing?" In my years of priesthood, very, very few Catholics and non-Catholics alike have said no. The majority were pleased and grateful, including those who professed to having little faith.

In blessings, graces are offered through the Church empowered by Jesus. Whether the graces are received depends upon the recipient. These graces can remit venial sins and assist the faithful in living out the grace received in the sacraments.

We can say that the grace of a blessing is offered when the individual who blesses has been recognized by the Church, empowered by Jesus, as one who can bless. Thus, the minister has the Church's intercession. It is this ecclesial institution and intercession that gives sacramentals their special efficacy with God. Of course, any pious act can be a moment of grace *ex opere operantis*, but sacramentals have the additional aspect of being instituted by the Church and graced through its intercession with God.[7] As canon lawyer John Paschang notes, "The minister acts in the name of the Church," and thus "it is the Church that blesses or consecrates."[8]

BLESSINGS CONTINUING JESUS' MINISTRY

As stated previously, blessings and sacramentals find their efficacy in the authority of the Church. As the *Catechism* notes, "Sacramentals are sacred signs instituted by the Church" (*CCC* 1677). Of course, this is true. Sacramentals receive their authority from the Church.

But blessings should not be completely separated from the ministry of Jesus. In reality, Jesus blessed many people. Whenever an individual was healed of a physical affliction, he or she was blessed *and* the physical infirmity was healed. Jesus' power was active in the miraculous catch of fish, and one might truly assert that the bounty of the fishermen's catch was a blessing from Jesus (see Jn 21:1–14). Jesus blessed the loaves and fishes, and thousands of people were fed (see Mt 14:13–21). Power emanated from the person of Jesus; the people and the world around him basked in that grace of the kingdom. They were blessed.

Jesus said that we who are his disciples are called to "do the works that I do, and will do greater ones than these" (Jn 14:12). I think it clear that when we as priests bless as he did, and in accord with his will, a grace is truly offered. It could be said that the power not only comes from the Church's authority, since we are commissioned to bless, but also from Jesus in imitation and continuation of his ministry.

We ought not to separate too sharply what the Church does in blessings and what Jesus did in blessings. In reality, the work of the Church seamlessly continues the work of Jesus through the power of the Holy Spirit. It is not two separate actions but one continuous action. The *Catechism* quotes the thought of St. Joan of Arc on this: "About Jesus Christ and the Church, I simply know they're just one thing, and we shouldn't complicate the matter" (*CCC* 795). We bless because Jesus did, and he commanded us to continue his work.

Blessing God's Creatures

It is time for us to revisit the question of whether objects or animals can be directly blessed. This question is important not only for the pastoral ministry of the Church but also for our understanding of the nature of the blessing.

The obvious answer to that question is yes. In reality priests have been blessing animals and objects for centuries: fields, animals, religious objects, meals, fruits of the fields, and more. The *Catechism of the Catholic Church* explicitly recognizes this: "Among sacramentals, blessings (of persons, meals, objects, and places) come first" (*CCC* 1671). So meals, objects, and places can be blessed.

The revised *Book of Blessings* seems to recognize this and includes orders for their blessing, such as the Order for the Blessing of Animals or the Order for the Blessing of Religious Articles. The title suggests that the thing is to be blessed. But the revised *Book of Blessings* does not actually have the minister blessing the animal or object directly but rather the people present. The animals and objects are thought to be blessed insofar as they contribute to the work of humans and God's plan for salvation history.

Nevertheless, I am reminded of the story a Catholic woman told me of how she selected her dog—or rather, how her dog selected her. She went to the home of an older woman who had advertised that she had a new litter of Bichon puppies ready for adoption. She went to the house, looked at the litter, and was about to choose one of the puppies, when the elderly lady stopped her and said, "No, the dog will choose you." So my friend sat on the floor some distance from the puppies. Eventually, one of them spied her and padded over to her and jumped into her lap. The two of them had a wonderful relationship of many years until the sad day of the Bichon's death. I cannot imagine telling someone such as this woman that on the Feast of St. Francis I would not be able to bless her dog directly.

When I asked an exemplary senior pastor if he blessed people's pets on St. Francis's feast day, he showed me a YouTube video that one of his parishioners had taken of him blessing pets. There he was in his stole and with holy water in hand, saying a blessing (from the revised *Book of Blessings*) and sprinkling holy water on a courtyard full of people and their pets, while the musicians sang "The Prayer of St. Francis." When I asked him if he actually blessed the animals themselves, he said, "Of course. They are God's creatures."

Indeed, they are God's creatures, and so we bless them. What does a blessing do for the animals? We know that blessings offer graced "spiritual effects" that help human beings live out their Christian lives with integrity. But what does a blessing do for an animal?

We might find the beginnings of an answer in the old ritual for the Blessing of Horses or Other Animals. The priest prays that the Lord will bless them "to the benefit of their being . . . and deliver them from all harm."[9] There is also a Blessing of Sick Animals. In this blessing the priest prays that the "animals afflicted with severe sickness may be cured."[10] In the Blessing of Cattle and Herds, the priest prays that God would "guard and watch over them."[11] There is an interesting Blessing of Silkworms in which the priest prays for them to "multiply."[12]

Given our previous biblical discussion, these prayers make sound theological sense. The Fall in Genesis precipitated illness and death. A sign of the coming kingdom of God, in which all of creation participates in some way, will include an eradication of disease and death. In these prayers, the priest's blessing, which is a grace that participates in the redemption of

Christ and the realization of the kingdom, prays for health and healing. And it prays for protection and multiplication, echoing the original blessing from God that people and animals would multiply and fill the earth.

Should we bless animals directly? I echo the sentiments of the senior pastor previously cited: "Of course. They are God's creatures." However, I also recommended to my pastor-friend that he not forget to bless the dogs' owners as well!

In blessing animals, we first thank and "bless" God. Then we bless the people for their sanctification and pray that they will exercise good stewardship over creation. Finally, we bless the animals since they are God's creatures.

One of the important elements of the post–Vatican II renewal of the sacramentals is its focus first on thanking or blessing God and then on the blessing of people. This is an important theological insight. Thus, in blessing animals, we ought first to give thanks and bless God for all these divine benefits. Then, we ought to bless the people present since they are called most directly to participate in the salvation of Christ. We also pray that they will exercise good stewardship over all of God's creation.

Finally, but without forgetting to do so, we bless God's creatures. As the liturgical reform noted, animals and objects are blessed because they contribute to the welfare of human beings and are taken up into God's salvation history. But the Church's long tradition also supports the pastoral practice of sprinkling the animals and objects themselves with holy water and praying that they be blessed directly. I personally see no conflict in both blessing animals and objects in their contributing to human welfare and their participation in salvation history, and also blessing them directly and praying for God's grace to descend upon them.

Talismans or Divine Blessings?

We should also look again at the blessing of religious objects such as rosaries, crucifixes, and religious medals. A consistent concern that had a significant impact on the post–Vatican II renewal of sacramentals was the fear of promoting superstition or magic. This is a special concern when discussing the blessing of religious objects.

The faithful have long believed that blessed religious objects have an apotropaic function (that is, warding off evil). Some of these practices likely grew out of old pagan beliefs and rituals. There are centuries-old pagan traditions of magic symbols and gestures being used to ward off evil. For example, nazars or large eyes were painted on drinking cups in sixth-century BC Greece to ward off the "evil eye." The evil eye was thought to be an effective curse people could use against others. Symbols of nazars are still popular in a myriad of countries today.

Gargoyles and other grotesque faces were carved into entryways to churches, thought by some to ward off evil spirits. One can see these on many older churches to this day. In a similar practice, near the end of the harvest season, frightening faces were carved into pumpkins, turnips, and beets to dispel the evil spirits believed to roam the earth on All Hallow's Eve, what we know as Halloween.[13] Even today we carve frightening faces into our pumpkins, but most are unaware of the practice's ancient roots and connection to warding off evil spirits.

Similarly, good-luck charms, rabbit's feet and amulets, knocking on wood, and crossing one's fingers are thought to bring good luck and divert evil influences. These all are evocative of pagan superstition. For instance, the lucky rabbit's foot may stem from a pagan belief that it was actually the foot of a shape-shifting witch that appeared in the form of a rabbit. The rabbit would have been killed in a cemetery during a particular phase of the moon.[14] Others associate rabbits with good fortune because of their great fertility. Regardless of the origin, such notions are not compatible with Christianity.

Clearly, the Catholic Church distances itself from such notions when blessing religious objects or any objects, but this does not mean we believe that everything about pagan cultures was bad. Many ancient pagans recognized the very real presence of evil in the world and the harm that evil could cause. They sought to protect themselves, their families, and their possessions from such harm. The belief in evil, and the desire to protect against it, were quite compatible with Christianity. However, pagan peoples did not recognize the true source of protection from evil, and so their practice might today be called a kind of "magic." Such practices could simply be ineffective or might actually make things worse if they invoked, consciously or unconsciously, other demonic powers.

Because of this fear of magical thinking, the revised *Book of Blessings* distances itself very far from such things. For example, in the Blessing of Religious Articles, after a catechetical introduction, reading of the Word, and intercessions, the priest or deacon prays (no lay ministers are authorized to bless religious articles):

BLESSING OF
RELIGIOUS ARTICLES (1989)

Blessed be your name, O Lord, you are the fount and source of every blessing, and you look with delight upon the devout practices of the faithful. Draw near, we pray, to these your servants and, as they use this symbol of their faith and devotion, grant that they may also strive to be transformed into the likeness of Christ your Son, who lives and reigns with you for ever and ever. Amen.[15]

However, the prayer does not actually mention blessing the religious objects themselves. Only God and the people present are blessed.

Similarly, in the Blessing of Rosaries, it is not the rosaries that are blessed directly, but instead the priest or deacon prays, "Send your blessing upon all who use these rosaries."[16] This apparent prohibition against blessing objects themselves is not absolute in the revised *Book of Blessings*. In the short blessing formulary for religious articles in general and rosaries in particular, the deacon or priest actually blesses both the object and the person who uses it. For example, over rosaries he prays, "May this rosary and the one who uses it be blessed."[17]

BLESSINGS AND EXORCISMS

It would certainly not be in keeping with centuries of Catholic tradition if religious objects themselves were thought to have no place in being a source of grace and protection for those who use them in faith. The religious objects themselves were blessed precisely because their use was thought to bring a special grace. For centuries, the pious have devoutly believed that it is not insignificant to have one's religious objects blessed; they continue to believe that there is a difference between a holy article that is blessed and one that is not.

Indeed, it appears that the Holy See believes this as well. The faithful are encouraged to bring their religious articles to the weekly papal audience to be blessed by the pope. The master of ceremonies announces in many languages, "At the end of the audience, the Holy Father will impart his apostolic blessing, which he willingly extends to the members of families at home. He intends to bless any religious articles which you may have brought for this purpose, and in a special way his blessing goes to your children and your loved ones who are sick." Then, the pope gives the standard pontifical blessing that every bishop uses at the end of the Mass.

This blessing by the Holy Father is a model for us. It is done in a liturgical context with a reading from scripture and prayer responses by the faithful present. The pope blesses not only the religious articles but also the people. He makes the Sign of the Cross at the end to signify that the blessing is imparted. This simple ceremony is rich in meaning and, no doubt, rich in the blessings of God.

Thus, we do bless religious objects. There is a difference between holy water and regular water, just as there is a difference between a blessed object and one that is not blessed. It is accepted that ordinary water can be used if necessary in Baptism. But some early authors spoke about the importance of blessing the water for Baptism.[18] St. Ambrose said, "Not all waters have a curative power: only that water has it which has the grace of Christ. There is a difference between the matter and the consecration, between the action and its effect. . . . The water does not heal unless the Spirit descends and consecrates the water."[19] Similarly, for Tertullian in his *Homily on Baptism*: "All waters, when God is invoked, acquire the sacred significance of conveying sanctity: for at once the Spirit comes down from heaven and stays upon the waters, sanctifying them from within himself, and when thus sanctified they absorb the power of sanctifying."[20] Also, for the fourth-century bishop Theodore of Mopsuestia in his *Baptismal Homily III*: "You are not baptized in ordinary water, but in the water of second birth. Now ordinary water cannot become this other thing except by the coming of the Holy Spirit. Consequently the bishop beforehand pronounced a prescribed form of words, asking God to let the grace of the Holy Spirit come upon the water and make it capable of begetting this awesome birth."[21]

Thus, blessed objects, especially those consecrated for liturgical use, should be cared for with suitable dignity. This also informed the early practice of the faithful taking home some of this consecrated water and using it to bless people and things. This is also why the laity know that, after purchasing a religious object, they should search out a priest to have it blessed.

The Church has long recognized the grace of sacramentals. To demonstrate the perceived effectiveness of sacramentals against evil, there is a long tradition of using sacramentals in exorcisms. It is clear that the Church believes such sacramentals have a powerful effect against the presence of evil.[22]

The Rite of Exorcism itself is a sacramental, and throughout the rite several other sacramentals are typically used. At one point, the exorcist holds up a crucifix and recites the ancient exorcistic formula: "*Ecce Crucem Domini, Fugite Partes Adversae*" ("Behold the Cross of the Lord; Be gone, all hostile powers").[23] The revised rite, as well as the older ritual, includes the crucifix as a sacramental designed to cast out the demonic presence.

Reflective of this theology of sacramentals, what first greets the pilgrim to St. Peter's Square in Rome are the large letters sculpted into the base of the obelisk under the crucifix in the center of the square: *Ecce Crux Domini, Fugite Partes Adversae*. In addition to its historic and artistic value, one would suppose that the placing of this crucifix and the exorcistic words in the center of St. Peter's Square is not a theological happenstance. Rather, it was meant to have an ongoing apotropaic and perhaps exorcistic function. Would not a blessed crucifix placed in faith in the household of believers have a similar function? Should not a priest or deacon encourage the faithful to display blessed crucifixes in their dwellings and places of work?

Similarly, holy water is an integral part of both the older and revised rites. The introduction to the official English translation of the Rite of Exorcism reads, "The rite begins with the sprinkling of holy water, by which, as a memorial of the purification received in Baptism, the troubled person is defended against the snares of the enemy."[24] When the water is blessed in the revised rite, the exorcist prays, "Pour forth into this water the power of your + blessing, that this your creature . . . may receive the power of divine grace to expel demons . . . [and] anything touched by this water may be freed from harm. Let not the evil spirit dwell there." Then he may add blessed salt. When he sprinkles the water, he may use the following words: "May this water be a memorial of the Baptism we have received."[25]

The revised rite links the Rite of Exorcism to Baptism. In addition to the use of holy water, which reminds one of Baptism, the rite includes a renewal of one's baptismal promises by renouncing Satan and professing one's faith. Also, the exorcist breathes on the possessed person, as a renewal of the Holy Spirit received in Baptism, and prays, "By the breath of your mouth, O Lord, drive out the evil spirits . . . for your kingdom is at hand."[26] So we see the post–Vatican II revision of the Rite of Exorcism, itself a sacramental, connecting an exorcism with a sacrament—namely, Baptism.[27]

The introduction to the Rite of Exorcism again mentions the ubiquitous contemporary caution, "The Exorcism should be performed in such a way that it manifest the faith of the Church and that no one can consider it as a magical or superstitious activity."[28]

As the exorcism continues, if holy water, crucifixes, or any other sacramental seems to the exorcist to be effective in a particular case of possession, the exorcist is encouraged to use it often throughout the sometimes-lengthy process of ridding the individual of a demonic presence.

Religious objects can have an apotropaic or exorcistic function. To avoid superstition, it is understood that (1) all power to cast out evil comes from God; (2) the power of religious objects comes through the intercession of the Church; and (3) such objects must be used in faith.

All of this suggests that the Church explicitly recognizes, as a result of centuries of experience, that sacramentals do indeed have a spiritual power to cast out evil. This would support St. Teresa of Avila's assertion that holy water is effective against evil. All of this also supports the pious use of sacramentals for their efficacy in warding off evil and being an instrument of blessings.

But what makes objects holy sacramentals, and not magical talismans, is, first, the recognition that it is ultimately the power of God that casts out evil. Second, these sacramentals find their efficacy in the intercession of the Church and not in some magical force or, worse, by invoking demonic powers. Third, these religious objects must be used in faith. So the use of sacramentals must be an act of Christian faith; otherwise, their use lapses into superstition.

When the farmer sprinkles holy water on his field or a pious couple puts a crucifix over their bed, the use of the sacramental is an act of faith. With the pious use of these sacramentals there is an actual graced effect offered. The presence of God's grace is a direct defense against evil.

BLESSINGS AS EXORCISMS

But should the act of blessing an object itself be a minor exorcism? Down through Church history, blessings became increasingly focused on casting out evil spirits. The renewed ritual after the Second Vatican Council included very little of this function. German theologian Reiner Kaczynski suggested that "the idea that blessings must be used to snatch created things from the power of the evil one and so purify them . . . in exorcisms" was an accretion of the Middle Ages that needed to be cast aside in the post–Vatican II liturgical reform.[29]

But the practice of blessings including an exorcism is actually an ancient one. It apparently evolved from the faithful taking home the holy water from the sacrament of Baptism. In the *Euchologion of Serapion of Thmuis* in the fourth century, there is a direct reference to the blessing of the water for Baptism with the faithful and then their taking this water for their own use at home. There is a reference to a sprinkling of holy water in a sixth-century redaction of the *Liber Pontificalis*. By the eighth century in the Gelasian Sacramentary of Rome, there is the Blessing of Water to Be Sprinkled in the Home, which is an exorcism and blessing of the water with exorcized salt added to it.[30]

From the early centuries on, Baptism included clear and prominent exorcistic and apotropaic elements. In AD 388, for example, St. John Chrysostom, in his address on Baptism, wrote, "After the renunciation of the devil and the covenant with Christ," the baptized person has "nothing in common with that evil one." He graphically described Satan as "that savage beast" and said that God holds "in check all the frenzy of the Evil One" because he has anointed the individual and "stamps thereon the sign of the cross." As a result of Baptism, "you will be secure and able to hold the serpent in check; you will suffer no harm."[31]

For some in this early period of Church history, Baptism was believed to literally include an exorcism, since it was considered that the newly baptized had previously been physically possessed by demons.[32] For example, in the beginning of the third century in Rome, the *Apostolic Tradition*, ascribed to Hippolytus, has rites for exorcizing candidates of evil spirits before they are baptized. The instructions state that those to be baptized are to be gathered on Saturday, "and when he lays his hand on them he shall exorcize them of every foreign spirit and they shall flee away from them and shall not return to them. And when he has finished exorcizing them he should blow on their faces; and when he has sealed their forehead, their ears and their noses he should make them stand up."[33] Blowing on the face was thought to have an exorcistic function.[34] Anglican priest and expert on early Church liturgy Alistair Stewart-Sykes commented on this passage: "The sealing is intended to seal up any entrances into which an evil spirit might attempt a return."[35]

For others, such exorcistic language was interpreted to mean that the newly baptized had been under the power of evil and sin until freed in Baptism but not that they were physically possessed. St. Augustine appears to be of the latter group, and although using exorcistic language at times, "he does not seem to have meant that the devil possessed them corporeally, however, but only that they had been subjected to his law as a result of original sin; their relationship to the devil was that of captive slaves to their master."[36] As time passed, more people came to believe as Augustine did, that these baptismal exorcisms were interpreted more symbolically as removing the newly baptized from Satan's dominion rather than as actual physical exorcisms.[37]

As noted previously in Ambrose and Tertullian, the water to be used in Baptism was thought to need a cleansing, perhaps an exorcism, if it would then be used to cleanse and sanctify those being baptized. For example, as previously cited, St. Cyprian wrote in his letter to Januarius, "It is required then that the water should first be cleansed and sanctified by the priest, that it may wash away by its baptism the sins of the one who is baptized."[38]

Around AD 700, the *Bobbio Missal* described the exorcism of baptismal water: "I exorcize you, creature of water . . . you whole army of the devil . . . be rooted out and put to flight from this creature of water."[39] In the Byzantine Rite, from a Greek manuscript circa AD 790, the priest blesses the water of Baptism by breathing into it and signing it with the cross three times as he prays: "May all the enemy powers be crushed down by the sign of the type of the cross of your Christ. May all aerial and unseen shapes depart from us, may no dark demon lie hidden in this water. . . . But, maker of all things, declare this water to be a . . . water of sanctification, a cleansing of the pollution of the body and soul . . . renewal of spirit, fount of life."[40]

Similarly, in the ninth century in Mainz, Germany, the archbishop's ritual included an exorcism of water. The celebrant prayed, "I exorcize you, creature of water," so that the water itself would be used for "driving away every power of the enemy; that you may be able to uproot and cast out the enemy himself with his apostate angels."[41] In a 1487 edition of the *Sarum Missal* of Salisbury, England, before the Sunday aspersion procession, the priest exorcized the salt and water.[42]

Thus, water was exorcized so that the water itself would then be used to cast out Satan. As cited previously from historian James Monti, the exorcizing of water and salt, which are then commingled to make holy water, was a "practice that became universal in the Middle Ages," but it began much earlier.[43]

The recent pre–Vatican II ritual included these kinds of exorcisms of water, oil, salt, and other objects. The exorcisms of salt and water were largely unchanged from the earliest examples of blessing water. Likewise, over the oil the priest prayed to dispel "the adversary's power, the devil's legions, and all Satan's attacks."[44] The use of exorcized oil is an ancient tradition in the Church, notably at Baptism. St. Cyril of Jerusalem in AD 350 described Baptism in this way, mentioning oil: "Next, after removing your garments you were rubbed with exorcized oil from the hair of your head to your toes, and so you became sharers in Jesus Christ."[45]

Why is it that blessings and sacramentals morphed from being used to cast out evil to the substances themselves needing first to be exorcized? As theologian Edward Yarnold, S.J., noted, "For the early Christians first the devil had to be driven out of the water by an exorcism, then the bishop invoked the Trinity to become present in the water."[46] To address this point, the Church continues to recognize that demons—that is, fallen angels and Satan—are real. One need only to read the *Catechism of the Catholic Church*, the documents of Vatican II, or the many references by Pope Francis[47] and the pontiffs before him (not to mention the gospels!) to realize that the existence of demons is clearly a part of the Catholic faith.

Second, from the same documents, it is clear that the reality of demons as present and active in our world is also part of our faith. But can they inhabit objects or nonhumans? When Jesus exorcized the man possessed by Legion, the demons went into the swine (see Lk 8:26–39). Also, in the revised Rite of Exorcism, there is a separate rite in the back of the book for exorcizing places: A Supplication and Exorcism Which May Be Used in Particular Circumstances of the Church. The introduction to this rite instructs, "The presence of the devil and other demons appears and exists not only in the tempting or tormenting of persons, but also in the penetration of things and places in some way by their activity."[48] So this revised post–Vatican II rite recognizes that demons can act in places and provides a ritual to expel them to be used under the guidance of the diocesan bishop.

But should one presume that the water and salt, and any other object exorcized, was actually infested by demons? I mentioned this to one exorcist, and he said he exorcizes water "just in case." But our theology does tell us that, despite creation's redemption in Christ, Satan is allowed a certain power in this world until the final consummation in Christ. All has been saved in Christ, and yet the kingdom is not yet here in its fullness. So it would seem appropriate to deliver everything from "Satan's power," the effects of sin, which are the final vestiges of his kingdom collapsing under the victory of Christ.

Varying approaches to the presence and influence of Satan and demons are still present today and remain a source of controversy. As in our day, some ancient authors understood these exorcisms over elements literally; they believed that demons were actually present in the elements. Other authors took this less literally and meant that all of creation is, in some way, under the influence of Satan until his power is fully exorcized. Still others interpreted this to mean that prayers and blessings had an apotropaic function and were thus simply a protection against evil. Some contemporary authors reject notions of any demonic influence over creation at all.

On the subject of the presence of personified evil and its influence, there is much disagreement.

In Appendix II of the current *Roman Missal*, we find a kind of middle ground. The celebrant prays for "protection . . . against all illness and every snare of the enemy" and also that "every attack of the enemy is repulsed."[49] Casting out and protecting against any Satanic influence and also redeeming creation in Christ are much in keeping with our tradition and theology. Exorcizing the water and salt is also a long-standing tradition. Perhaps explicitly casting out demons residing in the "creature of salt" might be more figurative than literal, but certainly delivering it from any evil influence would seem appropriate to this author.

So including an exorcistic element in blessings seems to be in harmony with our theology and ancient practice. At least, there should be an option of including such prayers in blessings. Pope Benedict XVI's *motu proprio, Summorum Pontificum* (2007), allowing the use of the older prayers, makes just such a provision. It allows a wider use of rituals that are of the *forma extraordinaria.*[50]

Nevertheless, such exorcisms ought to be placed in a balanced context. *A blessing is more than an exorcism.* At times, it appears that the two became almost equated, as if to bless is only to cast out evil. Rather, while recognizing the need to rescue all from the influence of evil, a blessing is more than eradicating evil. This is but another reason for the necessity of a post–Vatican II renewal of the sacramentals.

The instruction on the Lenten scrutinies of the elect gives us a good way to understand the relationship of exorcisms and blessings. These scrutinies in the RCIA program include an exorcistic element, and they may cause some to pause and wonder if they are but a relic of the past. However, the RCIA instruction says the following:

> For the scrutinies are celebrated in order to deliver the elect from the power of sin and Satan, to protect them against temptation, and to give them strength in Christ, who is the way, the truth and the life. These rites, therefore, should complete the conversion of the elect and deepen their resolve to hold fast to Christ and to carry out their decision to love God above all.[51]

It is the total process of conversion to move from the darkness into the light. The grace offered is both purifying and illuminating. "Renouncing

Satan and embracing Christ are really two parts of one action."[52] They cannot be separated.

If we lose the exorcistic element of blessings, we lose a sense of what we are converting from. And if we lose a sense of the illumination, then we may be moving out of the darkness, but we have no sense of where we are headed—namely, into the light of Christ. Some of the old rituals of blessings especially focused on the exorcism, while the revised *Book of Blessings* focuses strongly on Christ and the light. The Christian notion of conversion and the RCIA scrutinies bring these two aspects together into one movement, and so should our blessings. In our blessings, we need both aspects of moving out of the darkness and into the light.

Blessings ought to include both a movement out of the darkness and a movement into the light, both a protection from evil and an illumination with God's grace. Blessings are one unified act of converting creation into God's redeemed world.

A blessing praises God for his goodness and gifts. A blessing prays for the sanctification of the people present. A blessing prays that any objects to be blessed will be a source of divine grace and will be used in accord with God's plan of salvation. In addition to casting out the darkness, blessings open us to the light of God's kingdom.

It should be noted that some of the blessings in the pre–Vatican II ritual had no exorcistic element at all. So including such an element was not always thought to be essential for a blessing. Despite the differences between the older blessings and the revised blessings, I believe priests, acting under the leadership of their bishops, typically make up for any lacunae in the words of the prayers by their personal priestly ministry. The priest instinctively knows that in blessing something or someone, he finishes the blessing by extending his hands, making the Sign of the Cross, and saying, "May almighty God bless [X], the Father, and the Son, and the Holy Spirit." Surely, God's blessing is thus imparted, and God knows what is needed better than we.

I would add that the ministers of blessings and the people should not be overly scrupulous about the exact wording of a blessing. If a priest does not explicitly cast out the demons, does this mean they are not cast out by the blessing? No. When a priest or deacon or lay minister intends to bless and carries out the blessing according to the rites of the Church and under the authority of the local bishop, the needed grace is offered. Words certainly matter, but our God is not a parser of sentences.

The grace of God is abundant and effective. Of its very nature, God's grace reflects the simplicity of God, simultaneously casting out the darkness and illumining what is blessed. The power of the Spirit conforms the grace offered in the situation at hand to God's will. Otherwise, we could easily lapse into scrupulosity. The blessings of God should help us to trust even more in divine providence and love.

STRUCTURE AND SIGNS OF BLESSINGS

St. Augustine was one of the first to put forth the notion that sacraments are a combination of matter and form. Regarding holy water used in Baptism, he wrote, "Take away the word, and the water is neither more or less than water. The word is added to the element, and there results the Sacrament."[53]

Blessings are sacramentals and not sacraments; however, the same basic structure applies: blessings are usually a combination of some matter and form. Typically there is the person or object to be blessed, which is the matter, and then there is some sort of form, which is a combination of words and signs. When priests and people think of the form of a blessing, they usually think of the priest making a Sign of the Cross over the object or person and saying a prayer such as, "May almighty God bless [X], the Father, and the Son, and the Holy Spirit." The priest may lay hands on the object or person or add a sprinkling with holy water.

Since sacramentals are not sacraments, a specific form to be unerringly used is not essential for the blessing to be truly given, as is the case for sacraments. Limited modifications to fit the situation are allowed for sacramentals. However, to be valid and licit, the essential words and rite are to be followed. Over the centuries, some basic elements keep surfacing as constitutive of a blessing.

With the original publishing of the revised *Book of Blessings*, it became apparent that there were some blessings that did not explicitly include a Sign of the Cross. This became a source of controversy until it was resolved in a decree by the Congregation for Divine Worship and the Discipline of the Sacraments in September 2002. The decree said that every blessing by a bishop, priest, or deacon must have a Sign of the Cross.[54]

The Sign of the Cross is one of the very first signs of blessing used in the Church. It was used not only in liturgical rituals but also by the faithful in their daily lives. Tertullian (ca. AD 155 to ca. AD 240) wrote of its regular use by Christians: "Lastly, we make the sign of the cross on our foreheads at every turn, at our going in and coming out of the house, while putting on our shoes, when we are taking a bath, before and after meals, when we light the lamps, when we go to bed or sit down, and in all the ordinary actions of daily life."[55] Are we priests sufficiently catechizing our people to use regularly this powerful Christian symbol, the Sign of the Cross?

This decree by the Congregation is in harmony with the *Catechism of the Catholic Church*, which states, "They [sacramentals] always include a prayer, often accompanied by a specific sign, such as the laying on of hands, the sign of the cross, or the sprinkling of holy water (which recalls baptism)" (*CCC* 1668). It would seem to most priests and deacons that such signs typically make up the essentials of a blessing. Of course, the priest or deacon should have the intention to bless as well, but this is understood.

"They [sacramentals] always include a prayer, often accompanied by a specific sign, such as the laying on of hands, the sign of the cross, or the sprinkling of holy water (which recalls baptism)" (*CCC* 1668).

The revised *Book of Blessings* added additional elements that it said were important for blessings. Because a blessing is a liturgical action, some of the people should attend; the prayer should be spoken aloud; and there is a reading from the scriptures.[56] Again, the attempt was to guard against superstition and to make blessings actual liturgical celebrations.

The revised *Book of Blessings* offers a richer experience than many of the blessings in the old form and clearly promotes making it a liturgical event. Thus, the revised form implies the need for time to plan and execute the blessing. For example, if holy water is to be blessed, then it could easily be done in the context of a Mass or in a gathering of the faithful. Similarly, for blessing religious objects, could not the pastoral staff plan regular liturgical blessings in places of pilgrimage where the faithful often buy them? Typically, liturgical celebrations of blessings are already done on the great Feast of St. Francis for the blessing of the animals and on the Feast of St. Blase for the blessing of throats. There are other traditional liturgical blessings, such as the blessing of fields previously mentioned on Rogation Days. With a bit of planning and forethought, priests and deacons can organize these richer liturgical blessings to the edification and benefit of the community.

But what about the spontaneous requests such as "Bless my rosary" or "Father, please bless me"? Of course, we honor such spur-of-the-moment requests. Any seasoned cleric knows he must be flexible and open to the needs of the moment. Denying the heartfelt pleas for a blessing of someone in distress might seriously damage a person's connection to the Church or their faith. Yet these spontaneous pastoral encounters can be done in a way that is reverent and truly in the spirit of the Church's history of blessing. In fact, I have found these unplanned spontaneous encounters some of the most memorable in my years as a priest.

The General Instruction of the revised *Book of Blessings* seems to foresee such spontaneous events as including only the individual and the minister. It says, "Whenever there is no assembly of the faithful for the celebration, the person who wishes to bless God's name or to ask God's favor and the minister who presides should still keep in mind that they represent the Church in celebration." So the Church is present in these two people, reminiscent of the passage of scripture: "For where two or three are gathered together in my name, there am I in the midst of them" (Mt 18:20).[57]

Recently, I saw a woman approach the local bishop and ask him for his blessing. She bowed her head. Then, he reverently laid his hands on her head, closed his eyes, and prayed. It was a touching moment. Nothing was said aloud, but there was no doubt in anyone's mind that the woman received a wonderful blessing. This bishop is known for being a devout and kindly shepherd.

Even more to the point, I had the privilege of being in a small audience with Pope Francis. As the Holy Father walked from one person to the next, a very ill priest next to me was presented to him. The priest was in the final stages of cancer and looked ashen. He asked the Holy Father for his blessing. Pope Francis looked kindly at him and inquired gently about his illness. Then he laid his hands on the priest's head and prayed quietly. It was a moment of grace. Since then, this priest has passed on to the Lord, and he did so with the "imprint" of the hands of Peter and his blessing upon him.

While these spontaneous situations do not lend themselves to full liturgical expression, priests follow the teaching of the *Catechism* on blessings. They know that when they bless they use such signs as holy water, a Sign of the Cross, or the laying on of hands. They also know that, in that moment, they pray to God that this person may be blessed. In truth, in the act of blessing, the priest is acting *in persona Christi capitis*—he has become Christ looking into the eyes of the Father and imploring a special grace for this person. And the Father *never* refuses the prayer of the Son.

At the moment of blessing, the priest is Jesus looking into the eyes of his Father and asking for a special grace for this person. The Father *never* refuses the prayer of the Son.

SUMMARY

In this book, we have journeyed through the history and development of blessings. We started with the Old Testament, moved into the New Testament, and then down through two millennia of Church theology and praxis. Finally, we looked at the pre–Vatican II and the revised post–Vatican II *Book of Blessings*, as well as the theology of blessings today. During this journey, some important foundational principles emerged.

Sacramentals, of which blessings are first, ought to be an important part of the daily life of Christians. In a Catholic environment, we typically see many. There are crucifixes on walls, holy water fonts in our homes and churches, rosaries, scapulars, and more. Sacramentals in general, and blessings in particular, are important ways to sanctify the daily moments of our lives. The Seven Sacraments typically celebrate peak moments of human life, but sacramentals address our daily lives, reminding all the faithful that every part of our lives ought to be made sacred.

In pagan cultures, people sought out magical symbols, which they believed would ward off evil. Eschewing such magical notions, a foundational insight of the Old Testament tells us that all blessings and graces come from God, who is uniquely the Blessed One. The Israelites spontaneously looked to God to protect them from evil and to bless them and the work of their hands. They believed that if they remained faithful to God, he would bless them. But if they turned from his ways, they would ultimately end in ruin.

In the New Testament, Old Testament beliefs were assumed and transformed. Now, Jesus is recognized as the ultimate blessing. He is God's presence and the incarnation of every good. Moreover, the blessings he brings point to the kingdom and make this kingdom present. Jesus' greatest blessing is salvation—reconciliation with God and a sharing in his inheritance as adopted sons and daughters. In the witness of the New Testament, those most richly blessed are the poor in spirit, the meek, and those who suffer for the sake of the kingdom. As Jesus ascended to heaven, he blessed his disciples and empowered them to continue his ministry.

Priestly blessings and sacramentals arose very early in the life of the Church, but for centuries there was no clear distinction between sacramentals and sacraments. Rather, both were considered important moments of grace in which God granted his divine blessings and protections to the people.

Very early in the life of the Church, there grew the practice of the faithful taking home baptismal holy water and sprinkling it on themselves, their homes, their fields, and just about anything they wanted God to bless and protect. Crucifixes and other signs of the faith were thought to protect them from evil and to cast out demonic spirits. And the people earnestly beseeched the bishops and priests to bless them, their labors, their families, and their homes.

Interestingly enough, these pious practices arose not from the great councils or by papal decree as much as from the popular piety of the faithful. Blessings and sacramentals expressed and gave concrete shape to the faith of the People of God. They responded to the hopes and anxieties of the people of that day.[1] It is so today as well.

The growth and content of blessings reflect the faith and piety of the people. The Church continues to respond to their needs and sanctifies their daily lives with these sacramentals.

It might seem rather striking, but the popular piety of today is not so different from what it was more than a thousand years ago. People still recognize the dangers of traveling, so priests continue to bless ships, but now they bless cars and airplanes as well. Pregnancy, while far safer, remains an anxiety-provoking event, so priests bless pregnant mothers. Recently, a bishop told me that a young woman expecting twins asked him to "bless my belly." Exercising proper decorum, the bishop told her that he would be happy to do so but suggested that he bless "the whole person" and included her husband as well.

More than a few of the faithful in the twenty-first century want to be protected from harm, including from evil. They devoutly hang crucifixes and other holy objects where they live and work. The faithful continue to fill up their holy water containers and take them home to bless family, fields, and property, much as the faithful did in the early centuries of the Church. Some have decried such practices as medieval superstition, suggesting that these are remnants of pagan magical thinking. While it is true that the Church certainly needs to guard against magical or superstitious thinking, and the General Introduction to the revised *Book of Blessings* affirms the importance of proper catechesis to avoid "superstition and/or a shallow credulity,"[2] we should also be wary of an equally dangerous trend.

We priests can easily fall into a kind of patronizing clericalism in which we think the laity are theologically unsophisticated and need to be guided by our superior understanding. In reality, the priestly blessing and other sacramentals have been around since the earliest days of the Church and will remain long after this generation of bishops and priests is gone. If there is anything that deserves to be called an expression of the unerring *sensus fidelium*, affirmed by the Second Vatican Council, it is this steady piety of the faithful for two millennia.

The pre–Vatican II *De Benedictionibus* was an uneven collection of blessings gathered through the centuries. Moreover, in some cases, the blessings focused on the exorcistic function to the exclusion of the rich breadth of the meaning of God's blessings. It needed to be revised as the Council Fathers ordered. What emerged in the renewal were some important principles:

1. The Jewish notion of the *berakah* was recovered. It is God first who should be "blessed."
2. Then, the people present should always be blessed, even if the focus is on some religious object. We ought never to lose the opportunity to stretch out our hands in blessing people.
3. The renewal stressed the importance of blessings as a liturgical event and to include the participation of the faithful and a reading of the Word.

Throughout these renewed rituals, a sense of the richness of God's blessings emerges. But some important aspects of the older rituals ought to be recovered more fully. The question of whether objects or animals themselves can be blessed directly was raised in the renewal. As the General Introduction of the revised *Book of Blessings* reads, "Such blessings are invoked always with a view to the people who use the objects to be blessed."[3] Nevertheless, the long-standing practice in our tradition, until this very day, has been not only to bless the people but also to bless directly the animals and objects as well.

For example, in the thirteenth century St. Francis blessed the animals. The people continue to praise St. Francis's love and care for animals as they bring their own animals to church on October 4 to be blessed. Each week, Pope Francis blesses religious articles in St. Peter's Square. The people are very happy to have religious articles blessed by the pope. Could this all not be a sign of the *sensus fidelium*?

Also, from the beginning of Christianity, the people were rightly aware of Satan's activity in this world and sought God's protection. Including an apotropaic, and perhaps at times an exorcistic, element *should be* continued in blessings. The Church's teaching, coming straight from the words of Jesus, reminds us of the struggle against Satan present until the final age.

Moreover, the older ritual was more likely to include a sprinkling of holy water and a Sign of the Cross. Every priest instinctively knows that these remain important symbols in priestly blessings and are welcomed by the faithful.

Given the benefits of the revised *Book of Blessings* and the older ritual as well, it is happily the case that the priest can use either. As noted previously, Pope Benedict XVI's *motu proprio, Summorum Pontificum* (2007), allows the priest to use the former ritual as well.[4] A fine example of a blending of the new and the old is found in Appendix II of *The Roman Missal*. While predating the issuance of the revised *Book of Blessings*, the "Rite for the Blessing and Sprinkling of Water" has all the essential elements of a blessing. God is praised. The people are blessed. This sacramental is tied to the sacraments—specifically, the holy water is said to remind us of our Baptism. The water itself is blessed with a Sign of the Cross and mixed with exorcized salt (which is optional), over which the priest prays that "wherever this mixture of salt and water is sprinkled, every attack of the enemy may be repulsed." The priest prays that the water will be a source of forgiveness as well as protection "against all illness and every snare of the enemy."[5]

Regarding the actual wording of the blessings themselves, both the words used and the content of the prayers are important. The Old Testament understanding of the power of words reminds us of the importance of being careful about what we say and how it can affect the people and the world around us. Nevertheless, we ought not to be too scrupulous about mentioning everything in detail about what we want to happen as a result of the blessing. The latter would tend toward superstition. A prayer is an address to God, and he alone knows what is in our hearts and what graces are needed in that moment.[6] We do our best to give voice to the needs and hopes of the people, and God supplies the rest.

An exciting and hopeful change in the post–Vatican II renewal of Church blessings is an explicit and regular inclusion of deacons and the laity in blessings. The deacons have authority, much like priests, to bless people and objects. While deacons are not able to administer the sacrament of the Anointing of the Sick, there is an authorized Church blessing for the sick that they can preside over. It would be wise for deacons to make regular use of this sacramental during their hospital visits and sick calls. This ought not to substitute for the sacrament, but it can offer an important, healing grace.

Also, the Council Fathers recognized and formally approved that the laity have authority to bless "in special circumstances and at the discretion of the ordinary" (SC 79). There are a variety of circumstances in which they can bless. While they are not to extend their hands in blessing, as do the priests and deacons, the lay minister can trace a Sign of the Cross on people's foreheads, much as parents and godparents do during the baptismal rite.

In this regard, we priests need to do more instruction. The laity are largely unaware of these blessings and their role. We should especially encourage parents to bless their children on a regular basis, but most especially during important moments of their lives such as going off to school, engagement to be married, and the like. We can even encourage parents to give a nightly blessing to their children before sleep. Moreover, lay catechists are authorized and encouraged to bless their catechumens. The revised *Book of Blessings* includes other important blessings by the laity as well.

Pope Benedict XVI gave us a touching example of the importance of the blessing of parents. Into his old age he remembered well being blessed by his father and mother:

> I shall never forget the devotion and heartfelt care with which my father and mother made the sign of the Cross on the forehead, mouth, and breast of us children when we went away from home, especially when the parting was a long one. This blessing was like an escort that we knew would guide us on our way. It made visible the prayer of our parents, which went with us, and it gave us the assurance that this prayer was supported by the blessing of the Savior. . . . I believe that this blessing, which is a perfect expression of the common priesthood of the baptized, should come back in a much stronger way into our daily life.[7]

But presiding at blessings remains one of the long-recognized and central roles of the clergy. In fact, this is a custom that even predates the New Testament to the Old Testament, as is evident when one reads the book of Deuteronomy: "The priests, the descendants of Levi, shall come forward, for the LORD, your God, has chosen them to minister to him and to bless in the name of the LORD" (Dt 21:5). Here we see a clear reference to priests being consecrated to the Lord and given a special office of blessing the people. This long-standing tradition of seeking a priestly blessing is itself a faith-based recognition of God's salvation enacted through the Jewish people and continuing in New Testament times in Jesus. God has acted, and continues to act, through his Church, despite the many weaknesses of its clergy. When a stranger walks up to us, after seeing our Roman collar, and asks for a prayer, it is a faith-filled request and a belief that God has commissioned us to be instruments to bring his graces to the faithful. Such requests are, of course, always honored.

We ought not, nor is it possible, to compare the efficacy of priestly blessings to blessings of the laity. They are different in essence, not degree (*LG* 10; *CCC* 1592). But in the hierarchy of the Church, if a priest or deacon is present, the *Book of Blessings* is clear: he ought to preside. Of course, if a bishop is present, then he is the one to preside.

The revised *Book of Blessings* did not get into the issue of "powers" to bless. Also, the *Catechism of the Catholic Church* says, "Sacramentals derive from the baptismal priesthood" (*CCC* 1669). This is certainly true. However, the strong and clear tradition of the Church and the scriptures is that there is a "sacred power" to the ordained priesthood (*LG* 10).

In the Gospel of Luke it is said about Jesus: "Everyone in the crowd sought to touch him because power came forth from him and healed them all" (6:19). Since an ordained priest is uniquely configured to Christ, he continues the ministry of Jesus in a direct and unique way. This is expressed in the pre–Vatican II Rite of Ordination, when the bishop anoints the ordinand's hands with oil and prays, "What they bless shall be blessed."

The laity know this, and they intuitively look for a priest to bless them, their sacred objects, and their labors.[8] In recent years, the very human weaknesses of the clergy have been painfully splashed over the front page of newspapers around the world. It is our sins that they are publicizing, and so we have no recourse but to ask forgiveness. However, the laity still want a priest to bless them. Their desire is not a blindness to the weaknesses of the clergy but rather their recognition of priests' God-given sacred duties in sanctifying and blessing. Once again, we priests and bishops should be humbled by the faith of the laity who remain steadfast despite our wavering.

We priests greatly value and rightly focus much of our efforts on administering the Seven Sacraments. These are the great spiritual moments in people's lives. But as secularization sweeps the globe and becomes even more entrenched, fewer people are entering our churches. In the old days, priests spent much of their time in the church and in the rectories. The people usually came to them. Now, fewer come. We must now seek out the people.

The New Evangelization requires us to meet the people where they are. In the supermarkets, ball fields, schools, online, and more, the priest must find the people and engage them. One of the ways of ministering to them initially is through blessings. Not everyone will come to church, but many will be grateful for a blessing. This can be the beginning of an explicit faith journey for the recipient. Perhaps this "little" grace will open the doors of their hearts to God's more abundant blessings.

A short while ago, I was visiting in a nursing home and noticed a man in the room next to where I was visiting my sick mother. I said hello, and he invited me into his room. He was happy to have me visit. It turned out that the man was a lapsed Catholic and had a number of things he was angry about regarding the Church. I listened patiently and did not try to defend the Church. By the end of our visit, he seemed more open to my presence as a priest, and so I asked him, "Would you like to receive a blessing?" He said yes. I laid my hands on his head and blessed him. By the time I left, he seemed noticeably more at peace. I also found out that he had had three serious strokes recently, and his life was in the balance. While such blessings do not impart sanctifying grace per se, perhaps this small opening to God and his willingness to receive a blessing was a small mustard seed for the kingdom to take root in his life. Perhaps God was reaching out through a priest to offer this man healing and eternal life.

As we look out over the sea of humanity, many people are parched for the Word of Life, oftentimes unknown. No one is more acutely aware of this than our loving God, who pines even more than they do to shower his blessings on each and on all. Jesus has passed on to us priests the power and the authority to rain down God's blessings on the just and the unjust. May we not lose a moment or opportunity to be the instruments of God's generosity and mercy. And when we bless them, we too are blessed.

NOTES

PREFACE

1. *The Rites of Ordination*, in *The Roman Pontifical*, renewed by Decree of the Most Holy Second Ecumenical Council of the Vatican, Congregation for Divine Worship and Discipline of the Sacraments (Vatican City: Vox Clara Committee, 2012), section 124, p. 70.

1. THE GIFT OF BLESSINGS

1. *Origen: Homilies on Joshua*, trans. Barbara J. Bruce, ed. Cynthia White (Washington, DC: CUA Press, 2002), Homily 24:1, p. 205.

2. Daniel A. Machiela, *The Dead Sea Genesis Apocryphon: A New Text and Translation with Introduction and Special Treatment of Columns 13–17* (Boston: Brill, 2009), 77. "I laid my hands upon his [h]ead. Thus the affliction was removed from him, and the evil [spirit] driven away [from him]." See also Joseph A. Fitzmyer, *The Gospel according to Luke I–IX: A New Translation with Introduction and Commentary*, Anchor Bible, vol. 28 (Garden City, NY: Doubleday, 1982), 553.

3. Steven A. LaChance, *Confrontation with Evil: An In-Depth Review of the 1949 Possession That Inspired "The Exorcist"* (Woodbury, MN: Llewellyn Publications, 2017), 54.

4. A longer point of discussion would be the relationship of an exorcism to a blessing. A blessing and the Rite of Exorcism are both sacramentals. I believe that when a priest lays his hands on someone in blessing and when the exorcist "blesses" the possessed person, something similar, yet also different, happens. There is a powerful grace of God at work in both circumstances, but in different contexts and with different results.

Discussing the similarities and differences would be a fruitful discourse, yet beyond the scope of this current work.

5. Francis, Homily, December 13, 2016, in the *Catholic Register*, "Pope's Homily: Clericalism Distances the People from the Church," accessed May 23, 2018, https://www.catholicregister.org/faith/homilies/item/23834-pope-s-homily-clericalism-distances-the-people-from-the-church.

6. Derek A. Rivard, *Blessing the World: Ritual and Lay Piety in Medieval Religion* (Washington, DC: CUA Press, 2009), 277.

7. This is true in the traditional Filipino gesture of *mano*: the younger person takes the hand of an older, revered person and presses it to his or her forehead as a sign of respect and blessing. This is often done in that culture with Catholic priests as well.

8. Those usually coming up for a blessing at Communion time cross their arms over their chest, signaling to the priest to give them a blessing rather than the host. For my part, although it's not formally indicated in the ritual, I think it is a gentle pastoral way to deal with the increasing and serious problem of people coming up and receiving the Eucharist who should not be.

2. BLESSINGS IN THE OLD TESTAMENT

1. Magic does not recognize God as the source of all grace but rather seeks to personally control and manipulate preternatural and spiritual powers, often through rituals and spells thought to control these forces. There are many passages in the Bible forbidding such practices (e.g., Dt 18:9–12; 2 Kgs 21:6; Is 44:24–26).

2. Claus Westermann, *Blessing in the Bible and Life of the Church*, trans. Keith Crim (Philadelphia: Fortress Press, 1978), 119.

3. Eugene H. Maly, "Genesis," in *The Jerome Biblical Commentary*, ed. Raymond E. Brown et al. (Englewood Cliffs, NJ: Prentice-Hall, 1968), 11.

4. Josef Scharbert, "Blessing," in *Encyclopedia of Biblical Theology: The Complete Sacramentum Verbi*, ed. J. B. Bauer (New York: Crossroad, 1981), 69.

5. Derek A. Rivard, *Blessing the World: Ritual and Lay Piety in Medieval Religion* (Washington, DC: CUA Press, 2009), 26.

6. P. Jounel, "Blessings," in *The Sacraments*, vol. 3 of *The Church at Prayer: An Introduction to the Liturgy*, ed. A. G. Martimort et al. (Collegeville, MN: Liturgical Press, 1988), 264.

7. See also Sirach 15:16–17.

8. Scharbert, "Blessing," 72.

9. The Roman Ritual, *Book of Blessings*, Approved for Use in the Dioceses of the United States of America by the National Conference of Catholic Bishops and Confirmed by the Apostolic See (New York: Catholic Book Publishing, 1989), nos. 174–94, pp. 88–95.

10. *Book of Blessings*, no. 135, p. 73.

11. *Book of Blessings*, nos. 399–406, pp. 172–76.

12. *Book of Blessings*, no. 402, p. 174.

13. *Book of Blessings*, no. 175, p. 88.

14. Maly, "Genesis," 17.

15. Scharbert, "Blessing," 175.

16. Guy P. Couterier, "Jeremiah," in *Jerome Biblical Commentary*, 312.

17. Couturier, "Jeremiah," 313.

18. John L. McKenzie, *Dictionary of the Bible* (New York: Macmillan, 1965), 166.

19. John J. Castelot, "Religious Institutions of Israel," in *Jerome Biblical Commentary*, 727.

20. Edward Yarnold, *The Awe-Inspiring Rites of Initiation*, 2nd ed. (Collegeville, MN: Liturgical Press, 1994), 5.

21. Joseph Blenkinsopp, "Deuteronomy," in *Jerome Biblical Commentary*, 122.

22. R. Cabié, "Christian Initiation," in *The Sacraments*, 93: "According to the Apostolic Constitution *Divinae consortium naturae*, 'the laying of hands on the elect . . . is still to be regarded as very important, even if it is not of the essence of the sacramental rite [of Confirmation].' For ever since the Acts of the Apostles, Christians have regarded this gesture as a sign of the gift of the Spirit."

23. See Code of Canon Law, no. 1171: "Sacred objects, which are designated for divine worship by dedication or blessing, are to be treated reverently and are not to be employed for profane or inappropriate use even if they are owned by private persons." Accessed December 10, 2017, http://www.vatican.va/archive/ENG1104/_P48.HTM.

24. The Aaronic blessing may be found in the *Book of Blessings*, Appendix II, Solemn Blessings, no. 11, p. 875, and also in "Blessings at the End

of Mass and Prayers over the People," *The Roman Missal*, English Translation according to the Third Typical Edition, for Use in the Dioceses of the United States of America (Totowa, NJ: Catholic Book Publishing, 2011), 531.

3. Blessings in the New Testament

1. See also the Sermon on the Mount, Matthew 5:1–12.

2. Teresa of Calcutta, "Whatever You Did unto One of the Least, You Did unto Me," address at the National Prayer Breakfast, sponsored by the US Senate and House of Representatives, February 3, 1994, found at EWTN, accessed January 21, 2018, https://www.ewtn.com/library/issues/prbkmter.txt.

3. There is a striking example of a well-known journalist, using occult means, having admitted to trying to curse three people. Such actions are strongly condemned in the Christian tradition. See "DC Socialite Worries the Hexes She Put on People Might Have Killed Them," *Fox News*, September 14, 2017, http://www.foxnews.com/politics/2017/09/14/dc-socialite-worries-hexes-put-on-people-might-have-killed-them.html, accessed March 20, 2018.

4. This does not mean we have to approve of evil behavior. As traditional Catholic theology tells us, "Love the sinner but hate the sin." Unfortunately, there is much, much anger and ill will toward others today in and outside of the Church.

5. C. S. Mann, *Mark: A New Translation with Introduction and Commentary*, Anchor Bible, vol. 27 (Garden City, NY: Doubleday, 1986), 625.

6. Joseph A. Fitzmyer, *The Gospel according to Luke X–XXIV: A New Translation with Introduction and Commentary*, Anchor Bible, vol. 28A (Garden City, NY: Doubleday, 1985), 1199.

7. Manfred Hauke, "The Theological Battle over the Rite of Exorcism, 'Cinderella' of the New *Rituale Romanum,*" *Antiphon* 10, no. 1 (2006): 35.

8. Josef Scharbert, "Blessing," in *Encyclopedia of Biblical Theology: The Complete Sacramentum Verbi*, ed. J. B. Bauer (New York: Crossroad, 1981), 74. Like Jesus, Mary is also called *eulogēmenoi*. The only other use of this word, in addition to Jesus and Mary, refers to Jesus' kingdom (see Mk 11:10) and to his redeemed disciples (Mt 25:34).

9. *New American Bible*, St. Joseph Edition (New York: Catholic Book Publishing, 1970); see footnote for John 12:13 on p. 165.

10. Fitzmyer, *The Gospel according to Luke X–XXIV*, 1037.

11. Claus Westermann, *Blessing in the Bible and Life of the Church*, trans. Keith Crim (Philadelphia: Fortress Press, 1978, 77.

12. As quoted in Westermann, *Blessing in the Bible and Life of the Church*, 84.

13. "Interview with Pope Francis," *La Stampa*, May 29, 2014, http://www.lastampa.it/2014/05/27/vaticaninsider/eng/the-vatican/abusing-a-minor-is-like-celebrating-a-black-mass-DQDzTODROXYVqqZO-jFrjmJ/pagina.html, accessed May 23, 2018.

14. Joseph A. Fitzmyer, *The Gospel according to Luke I–IX: A New Translation with Introduction and Commentary*, Anchor Bible, vol. 28 (Garden City, NY: Doubleday, 1981), 768.

15. Fitzmyer, *The Gospel according to Luke I–IX*, 768.

16. The Roman Ritual, vol. 3, *The Blessings*, trans. and ed. Philip T. Weller (Milwaukee: Bruce Publishing, 1946), 469.

17. The Roman Ritual, *Book of Blessings,* Approved for Use in the Dioceses of the United States of America by the National Conference of Catholic Bishops and Confirmed by the Apostolic See (New York: Catholic Book Publishing, 1989), no. 1033, p. 440.

18. *Book of Blessings*, no. 1033, p. 440.

19. As quoted in Westermann, *Blessing in the Bible and Life of the Church*, 84.

4. A History of Blessings in the Church

1. John L. Paschang, *The Sacramentals according to the Code of Canon Law* (Washington, DC: Kessinger Legacy Reprints, 1925), 28.

2. Keith E. Kenney, "A Theology of Blessings," Spring 2014, unpublished. Cited with permission.

3. Henri Leclercq, "Sacramentals," in *The Catholic Encyclopedia*, vol. 13 (New York: Robert Appleton, 1912), as cited at New Advent, accessed May 26, 2018, http://www.newadvent.org/cathen/13292d.htm. "Apart from the ceremonies relating to the administration of the sacraments the Church has instituted others for the purpose of private devotion. To distinguish between them, the latter are named sacramentals because of the resemblance between their rites and those of the sacraments properly so-called. In ancient times the term sacrament alone was used, but numerous confusions resulted and the similarity of rites and terms led many Christians

to regard both as sacraments. After Peter Lombard the use and definition of the word 'sacramental' had a fixed character and was exclusively applicable to those rites presenting an external resemblance to the sacraments but not applicable to the sensible signs of Divine institution. St. Thomas Aquinas makes use of the terms sacra and sacramentalia (Summa I-II, Q. cviii, a. 2 ad 2um; III, Q. lxv, a. 1 ad 8um), which the theologians of a later period adopted, so that at present sacramentalia is exclusively reserved for those rites which are practiced apart from the administration of the seven sacraments." See also Kenney, "A Theology of Blessings," 8–9. Also see Paschang, *Sacramentals*, 4–5.

4. Derek A. Rivard, *Blessing the World: Ritual and Lay Piety in Medieval Religion* (Washington, DC: CUA Press, 2009), 39.

5. Rivard, *Blessing the World*, 40.

6. Philip T. Weller, "Introduction," in The Roman Ritual, vol. 3, *The Blessings*, trans. and ed. Philip T. Weller (Milwaukee: Bruce Publishing, 1946), x; Kenney, "A Theology of Blessings," 5.

7. Henry Theiler, *Holy Water and Its Significance for Catholics*, trans. Rev. J. F. Lang (New York: Fr. Pustet, 1909), chap. 2, Kindle.

8. Weller, "Introduction," xi.

9. Weller, "Introduction," xii.

10. The Roman Ritual, *The Order of Celebrating Matrimony*, English Translation according to the Second Typical Edition, for Use in the Dioceses of the United States of America, Approved by the United States Conference of Catholic Bishops and Confirmed by the Apostolic See (Collegeville, MN: Liturgical Press, 2016), 22.

11. Claus Westermann, *Blessing in the Bible and Life of the Church*, trans. Keith Crim (Philadelphia: Fortress Press, 1978), 105–6.

12. Westermann, *Blessing in the Bible and Life of the Church*, 106–7.

13. Rivard, *Blessing the World*, 27.

14. Westermann, *Blessing in the Bible and Life of the Church*, 106–8. Such blessings are often bookends in the Pauline letters as well. For example, 2 Corinthians opens with a blessing, "Grace to you and peace from God our Father and the Lord Jesus Christ" (1:2), and closes with one as well, "The grace of the Lord Jesus Christ and the love of God and the fellowship of the holy Spirit be with all of you" (13:13). Of course, Pauline blessings are strongly Christological.

15. Rivard, *Blessing the World*, 38–39.

16. Reiner Kaczynski, "Blessings in Rome and the Non-Roman West," in *Sacraments and Sacramentals: Handbook for Liturgical Studies*, vol. 4, ed. Anscar J. Chupungco (Collegeville, MN: Liturgical Press, 2000), 408.

17. Rivard, *Blessing the World*, 29.

18. Kaczynski, "Blessings in Rome and the Non-Roman West," 400–401.

19. E. C. Whitaker, *Documents of the Baptismal Liturgy*, revised by Maxwell E. Johnson (Collegeville, MN: Liturgical Press, 2003), 12.

20. James Monti, *A Sense of the Sacred: Roman Catholic Worship in the Middle Ages* (San Francisco: Ignatius Press, 2012), 95; see also Whitaker, *Documents of the Baptismal Liturgy*, 125–27.

21. Kaczynski, "Blessings in Rome and the Non-Roman West," 401.

22. Alistair Stewart-Sykes asserts that the *Apostolic Tradition* was indeed a third-century document. However, he believes it was the product of a community, with Hippolytus being "the last in a series of figures who 'wrote' *Apostolic Tradition.*" See Alistair Stewart-Sykes, *On the Apostolic Tradition*, an English Version with Introduction and Commentary (Crestwood, NY: St. Vladimir's Seminary Press, 2001), 11. Whitaker states that the *Apostolic Tradition* "may well reflect a synthesis or composite text of various and diverse liturgical patterns and practices . . . some quite early, others not added until the time of its final redaction" (Whitaker, *Documents of the Baptismal Liturgy*, 4).

23. *The Apostolic Tradition of Hippolytus*, trans. Burton Scott Easton (Cambridge: Cambridge University Press, 1962), 52, found at Rore Sanctifica, accessed May 25, 2018, http://www.rore-sanctifica.org/bibliotheque_rore_sanctifica/12-pretendue_tradition_apostolique_d_hippolyte/1934-burton_scott_easton-tradition_apostolique_d_hippolyte/Burton_Scott_Easton_-_The_Apostolic_Tradition_of_Hippolytus_(1934).pdf. See also Stewart-Sykes, *On the Apostolic Tradition*, 149.

24. As Stewart-Sykes notes, "It is hard to discern the basis behind the particular fruits which are to be offered for blessing and those to be refused." He then goes on to give some possible explanations from rabbinic writings. See Stewart-Sykes, *On the Apostolic Tradition*, 150–51.

25. Stewart-Sykes, *On the Apostolic Tradition*, 149.

26. Monti, *A Sense of the Sacred*, 15.

27. Rivard, *Blessing the World*, 219–26.

28. The Roman Ritual, *Book of Blessings,* Approved for Use in the Dioceses of the United States of America by the National Conference of

Catholic Bishops and Confirmed by the Apostolic See (New York: Catholic Book Publishing, 1989), no. 1985, p. 841.

29. As cited in Rivard, *Blessing the World*, 161.

30. "Bishop Resists Naming a Sub Corpus Christi," *Washington Post*, November 26, 1981, https://www.washingtonpost.com/archive/politics/1981/11/26/bishop-resists-naming-a-sub-corpus-christi/b8cf3981-9301-4ba7-a965-ccbe7b1246de/?utm_term=.8e733b598a52. The submarine, SSN705, was eventually named the *City of Corpus Christi* in an attempt to respond to the concerns expressed about its name. The submarine was officially decommissioned on August 3, 2017; see US Carriers, accessed January 11, 2018, http://www.uscarriers.net/ssn705history.htm.

31. "Bishop Resists Naming a Sub Corpus Christi," *Washington Post*, November 26, 1981.

32. Fr. Vincent Capodanno Biography, Archdiocese of the Military Services USA, accessed December 16, 2017, http://www.milarch.org/father-capodanno-bio.

33. USS *Capodanno*, Navsource Online: Destroy Escort Photo Archive, accessed December 16, 2017, http://www.navsource.org/archives/06/06021093.htm.

34. Kaczynski, "Blessings in Rome and the Non-Roman West," 401.

35. John Paul II, *Redemptor Hominis* (March 4, 1979), no. 15, http://w2.vatican.va/content/john-paul-ii/en/encyclicals/documents/hf_jp-ii_enc_04031979_redemptor-hominis.html.

36. Francis, *Laudato Si'* (May 24, 2015), no. 68, http://w2.vatican.va/content/francesco/en/encyclicals/documents/papa-francesco_20150524_enciclica-laudato-si.html.

37. Francis of Assisi, *The Canticle of the Creatures*, found at Custodia Terrae Sanctae, accessed December 29, 2017, http://www.custodia.org/default.asp?id=1454.

38. Kevin Irwin, "A Sacramental World: Sacramentality as the Primary Language for Sacraments," *Worship* 76, no. 3 (May 2002): 198.

39. Irwin, "A Sacramental World," 199.

40. *New American Bible*, St. Joseph's Edition (New York: Catholic Book Publishing, 1992); see footnote for Genesis 2:8.

41. David Power, "On Blessing Things," in *Blessing and Power*, ed. Mary Collins and David Power (Edinburgh: T and T Clark, 1985), 31. See also Rivard, *Blessing the World*, 135: "Blessings were thus used to transform

ordinary moments of sensible life into contact with the divine, to turn common items into things holy."

42. Irwin, "A Sacramental World," 205.

43. Irwin, "A Sacramental World," 205.

44. Frederick L. Moriarty, "Isaiah 1–39," in *The Jerome Biblical Commentary*, ed. Raymond E. Brown et al. (Englewood Cliffs, NJ: Prentice-Hall, 1968), 273.

45. Weller, The Roman Ritual, vol. 3, *The Blessings*, 9–11.

46. Rogation Days in the United States are also referred to by the USCCB Secretariat for Divine Worship in its July 2016 newsletter as "Days of Prayer." "These are occasions in which the national or local Church focuses its prayers and works toward a specific intention." See Divine Worship, USCCB, accessed January 30, 2018, http://www.usccb.org/about/divine-worship/newsletter/upload/newsletter-2016-07.pdf.

47. Jim Moore, "#TBT Rogation Days: Asking God for Protection throughout the Year," Aquinas and More, accessed December 16, 2017, http://www.aquinasandmore.com/blog/tbt-rogation-days-asking-god-for-protection-throughout-the-year.

48. Weller, The Roman Ritual, vol. 3, *The Blessings*, 357.

49. Weller, The Roman Ritual, vol. 3, *The Blessings*, 357.

50. Weller, The Roman Ritual, vol. 3, *The Blessings*, 359.

51. Weller, The Roman Ritual, vol. 3, *The Blessings*, 359.

52. *Book of Blessings*, nos. 981, 983, p. 423.

53. *Book of Blessings*, no. 26, p. 28.

54. *Book of Blessings*, no. 982, p. 423.

55. "Prayers to Care for Creation," Prayer and Worship, USCCB, accessed December 16 2017, http://www.usccb.org/prayer-and-worship/prayers-and-devotions/prayers/prayers-to-care-for-creation.cfm.

56. "Prayers to Care for Creation," Prayer and Worship, USCCB, accessed December 16 2017, http://www.usccb.org/prayer-and-worship/prayers-and-devotions/prayers/prayers-to-care-for-creation.cfm.

57. "Prayers to Care for Creation," Prayer and Worship, USCCB, accessed December 16 2017, http://www.usccb.org/prayer-and-worship/prayers-and-devotions/prayers/prayers-to-care-for-creation.cfm.

58. Monti, *A Sense of the Sacred*, 633.

59. Monti, *A Sense of the Sacred*, 633.

60. Monti, *A Sense of the Sacred*, 633.

61. C. S. Mann, *Mark: A New Translation with Introduction and Commentary*, Anchor Bible, vol. 27 (Garden City, NY: Doubleday, 1986), 275; and Joseph A. Fitzmyer, *The Gospel according to Luke I–IX: A New Translation with Introduction and Commentary*, Anchor Bible, vol. 28 (Garden City, NY: Doubleday, 1981), 546.

62. Rivard, *Blessing the World*, 54.

63. Monti, *A Sense of the Sacred*, 635.

64. Monti, *A Sense of the Sacred*, 637–38.

65. Weller, The Roman Ritual, vol. 3, *The Blessings*, 163, 165.

66. *Book of Blessings*, no. 2008, p. 850.

5. THE *BOOK* OF *BLESSINGS*

1. Uwe Michael Lang, "Theologies of Blessing: Origins and Characteristics of *De benedictionibus* (1984)," *Antiphon* 15, no. 1 (2011): 27–28.

2. Lang, "Theologies of Blessing," 30.

3. Daniel G. Van Slyke, "The Order for Blessing Water: Past and Present," *Antiphon* 8, no. 2 (2003): 15.

4. Lang, "Theologies of Blessing," 33.

5. The Roman Ritual, *Book of Blessings,* Approved for Use in the Dioceses of the United States of America by the National Conference of Catholic Bishops and Confirmed by the Apostolic See (New York: Catholic Book Publishing,1989), no. 19, p. 27.

6. Lang, "Theologies of Blessing," 35.

7. Reiner Kaczynski, "Blessings in Rome and the Non-Roman West," in *Sacraments and Sacramentals: Handbook for Liturgical Studies*, vol. 4, ed. Anscar J. Chupungco (Collegeville, MN: Liturgical Press, 2000), 400.

8. *Book of Blessings*, no. 1396, p. 595.

9. The Roman Ritual, vol. 3, *The Blessings*, trans. and ed. Philip T. Weller (Milwaukee: Bruce Publishing, 1946), 261.

10. Kaczynski, "Blessings in Rome and the Non-Roman West," 403.

11. *Book of Blessings*, no. 23, p. 28.

12. Kaczynski, "Blessings in Rome and the Non-Roman West," 401.

13. *Book of Blessings*, no. 17, p. 25.

14. P. Jounel, "Blessings," in *The Church at Prayer: An Introduction to the Liturgy*, vol. 3, *The Sacraments*, ed. A. G. Martimort et al. (Collegeville, MN: Liturgical Press, 1988), 264.

15. *Book of Blessings*, no. 847, p. 369.

16. *Book of Blessings*, no. 12, p. 24.

17. As cited in Ryan T. Ruiz, *Inclinate Vos Ad Benedictionem: A Study of the Theological, Pastoral and Cultural Implications of Aptatio/Inculturatio in the Church's Post-Conciliar Rites of Blessing* (Rome: Pontificium Athenaeum S. Anselmi De Urbe, 2016), 11.

18. Kaczynski, "Blessings in Rome and the Non-Roman West," 403.

19. Cardinal Noè gave an inspiring description of their last meeting: "However what I remember most clearly of that last meeting with Don Achille were his eyes, I had never seen them so large and luminous. In a way, those eyes were ready to contemplate the liturgy of heaven." "In Memoriam," Vatican News Services, July 7, 2006, accessed May 28, 2018, http://www.vatican.va/news_services/liturgy/2006/documents/ns_lit_doc_20060707_in-memoriam_en.html.

20. Van Slyke, "The Order for Blessing Water: Past and Present," 17.

21. Keith Edward Kenney, "A Theology of Blessings," Spring 2014, unpublished. Cited with permission.

22. Alex Stock, "The Blessing of the Font in the Roman Liturgy," in *Concilium: Blessing and Power* 178, no. 2 (1985): 43–44.

23. Weller, The Roman Ritual, vol. 3, *The Blessings*, 329.

24. *Book of Blessings*, no. 957, pp. 414–15.

25. *Book of Blessings*, nos. 942–65, pp. 409–15.

26. Weller, The Roman Ritual, vol. 3, *The Blessings*, 329.

27. *Book of Blessings*, no. 955, p. 413.

28. *Book of Blessings*, no. 955, p. 413.

29. Derek A. Rivard, *Blessing the World: Ritual and Lay Piety in Medieval Religion* (Washington, DC: CUA Press, 2009), 78. See also *The Gelasian Sacramentary, Liber Sacramentorum Romanae Ecclesiae*, ed. H. A. Wilson (Oxford: Clarendon Press, 1894), III: LXXV, p. 285, found at US Archive, accessed January 20, 2018, https://ia902701.us.archive.org/7/items/gelasiansacrame00gelagoog/gelasiansacrame00gelagoog.pdf.

30. Carol Macmurrough, "The Blessing of Homes: Roman Rite," *Orate Fratres* 14, no. 5 (March 17, 1940): 203.

31. Weller, The Roman Ritual, vol. 3, *The Blessings*, 73.

32. Weller, The Roman Ritual, vol. 3, *The Blessings*, 241.

33. Weller, The Roman Ritual, vol. 3, *The Blessings*, 39–43, 73.

34. Weller, The Roman Ritual, vol. 3, *The Blessings*, 241, 243.

35. *Book of Blessings*, no. 660, p. 291.

36. *Book of Blessings*, no. 673, p. 296.

37. *Book of Blessings*, no. 675, p. 296.

38. *Book of Blessings*, no. 663, p. 291.

39. Weller, The Roman Ritual, vol. 3, *The Blessings*, 241.

40. Code of Canon Law, no. 1170, accessed December 15, 2017, http://www.vatican.va/archive/ENG1104/_P48.HTM.

6. Holy Water

1. Derek A. Rivard, *Blessing the World: Ritual and Lay Piety in Medieval Religion* (Washington, DC: CUA Press, 2009), 62.

2. *Apostolic Constitutions,* Book VII, Concerning Deportment, and the Eucharist, and Initiation into Christ, XLIII, "A Thanksgiving concerning the Mystical Water," accessed December 16, 2017, https://ldsfocuschrist2.files.wordpress.com/2012/03/apostolic-constitutions-william-whiston.pdf.

3. *The Gelasian Sacramentary: Liber Sacramentorum Romanae Ecclesiae*, ed. H. A. Wilson (Oxford: Clarendon Press, 1894), III: LXXV, p. 285, found at US Archive, accessed January 20, 2018, https://ia902701.us.archive.org/7/items/gelasiansacrame00gelagoog/gelasiansacrame00gelagoog.pdf.

4. James Monti, *A Sense of the Sacred: Roman Catholic Worship in the Middle Ages* (San Francisco: Ignatius Press, 2012), 95; see also *Gelasian Sacramentary*, III: LXXV–LXXVI.

5. For a discussion of the relationship of exorcisms to blessings in the Gallican and Roman liturgies, see Dominic Serra, "The Blessing of Baptismal Water at the Paschal Vigil: Ancient Texts and Modern Revisions," *Worship* 64 (1990): 145, 142.

6. Hincmar of Reims, *Chapters Given to Priests*, chap. 5, *Patrologia Latina* 125, col. 774, as cited in Monti, *A Sense of the Sacred*, 96.

7. The Roman Ritual, *Rite of Baptism for Children*, Approved for Use in the Dioceses of the United States of America, Revised by the Decree of the Second Vatican Council (New York: Catholic Book Publishing, 1969), no. 54, pp. 36–37.

8. The Roman Ritual, vol. 3, *The Blessings*, trans. and ed. Philip T. Weller (Milwaukee: Bruce Publishing, 1946), 11.

9. The Roman Ritual, *Book of Blessings,* Approved for Use in the Dioceses of the United States of America by the National Conference of

Catholic Bishops and Confirmed by the Apostolic See (New York: Catholic Book Publishing, 1989), no. 17, p. 25.

10. *Book of Blessings*, no. 1396, p. 595.

11. *The Roman Missal*, Appendix II: "Rite for the Blessing and Sprinkling of Water," English Translation according to the Third Typical Edition, for Use in the Dioceses of the United States of America, Approved by the USCCB and Confirmed by the Apostolic See (Totowa, NJ: Catholic Book Publishing, 2011), 1298.

12. *The Roman Missal*, Appendix II: "Rite for the Blessing and Sprinkling of Water," 1296.

13. Teresa of Avila, *The Life of Teresa of Jesus*, trans. and ed. E. Allison Peers, chap. 31, p. 173, found at Carmelite Monks, accessed December 16, 2017, http://www.carmelitemonks.org/Vocation/teresa_life.pdf.

14. As cited in Monti, *A Sense of the Sacred*, 620.

15. Monti, *A Sense of the Sacred*, 620.

16. "Thou shalt not procure abortion." *Didache,* chap. 2, no. 2, accessed December 16, 2017, http://www.thedidache.com.

17. From the Codex Vindobonensis Palatinus, as cited in Monti, *A Sense of the Sacred*, 621.

18. *Book of Blessings*, no. 228, p. 106.

19. *Book of Blessings*, no. 229, p. 107.

7. WHO CAN BLESS?

1. *The Apostolic Tradition of Hippolytus*, trans. Burton Scott Easton (Cambridge: Cambridge University Press, 1962), 43, found at Rore Sanctifica, accessed May 25, 2018, http://www.rore-sanctifica.org/bibliotheque_rore_sanctifica/12-pretendue_tradition_apostolique_d_hippolyte/1934-burton_scott_easton-tradition_apostolique_d_hippolyte/Burton_Scott_Easton_-_The_Apostolic_Tradition_of_Hippolytus_(1934).pdf.

2. Spirit Daily, accessed December 16, 2017, http://www.spiritdaily.net/laymenexorcisms.htm.

3. See Ryan T. Ruiz, *Inclinate Vos Ad Benedictionem: A Study of the Theological, Pastoral and Cultural Implications of Aptatio/Inculturatio in the Church's Post-Conciliar Rites of Blessing* (Rome: Pontificium Athenaeum S. Anselmi De Urbe, 2016), 127. Fr. Ruiz summarized the first rule in the introduction to the 1614 Roman Ritual's section *De Benedictionibus*: "The

introductory section, *Regulae generales,* is brief, with six rules regulating the celebration of the orders of blessing. The first rule is a juridical affirmation of the priest's competency to be minister of the blessings contained within the liturgical book. This rule reads that 'the priest shall have made himself familiar with the blessings of these things which pertain to himself, and those which pertain to the bishop by right, so as not to usurp rashly the rights of someone of greater dignity [the bishop], or to take [from the bishop] his own authority out of ignorance.' The priest is clearly understood to be a legitimate minister of blessings, but his power to bless is always done in close cooperation with the bishop."

4. Code of Canon Law, no. 1168, accessed December 16, 2017, http://www.vatican.va/archive/ENG1104/_P48.HTM.

5. The revised *Book of Blessings* stipulates that "an acolyte or a reader who by formal institution has this special office is rightly preferred over another layperson as the minister designed at the discretion of the local Ordinary to impart certain blessings," no. 18, p. 26.

6. The Roman Ritual, *Book of Blessings,* Approved for Use in the Dioceses of the United States of America by the National Conference of Catholic Bishops and Confirmed by the Apostolic See (New York: Catholic Book Publishing, 1989), no. 18, p. 26.

7. *Book of Blessings*, nos. 392, 394, pp. 170–71.

8. *Book of Blessings*, no. 57, p. 40.

9. *Book of Blessings*, nos. 150, 166, 172, pp. 78, 84, 86.

10. For a short biography of Lanfranc of Pavia, see Wikipedia, accessed January 13, 2018, https://en.wikipedia.org/wiki/Lanfranc.

11. As cited in Derek A. Rivard, *Blessing the World: Ritual and Lay Piety in Medieval Religion* (Washington, DC: CUA Press, 2009), 43.

12. Pierre de Puniet, O.S.B., *The Roman Pontifical: A History and Commentary* (New York: Longmans, Green, 1932), 236.

13. Puniet, *The Roman Pontifical: A History and Commentary*, 234.

14. *The Rites of Ordination* in The Roman Ritual and Pontifical, no. 133, p. 80.

15. *Book of Blessings*, no. 1444, p. 617.

16. *Book of Blessings*, no. 18, p. 26.

17. Benedict XVI, *Omnium in Mentem* (October 26, 2009), http://w2.vatican.va/content/benedict-xvi/en/apost_letters/documents/hf_ben-xvi_apl_20091026_codex-iuris-canonici.html.

18. Congregation for the Doctrine of the Faith, "Note on the Minister of the Anointing of the Sacrament of the Sick" (February 11, 2005), http://www.vatican.va/roman_curia/congregations/cfaith/documents/rc_con_cfaith_doc_20050211_unzione-infermi_en.html (accessed 1/13/18).

19. *Book of Blessings*, no. 378, p. 163.

20. *Book of Blessings*, no. 392, p. 170.

21. *Book of Blessings*, no. 406, p. 176.

22. This was the position taken by Anthony Vanderhaar, as cited in Fr. George Stuart's Canon Law dissertation, "The Meaning of Sacred Status in the 1917 and 1983 Codes of Canon Law" (Catholic University of America, 2001), 98: "So he [Vanderhaar] posited two sources for the ability to receive delegation to administer sacramentals, one based on priestly ordination, and one based on a 'mandate from the community.' He concluded that when a priest administers sacramentals, it is due 'proximately to his union with the community but ultimately to his special union with Christ brought by his character. Other Christians who may on occasion administer the sacramentals do not do so by participating in the power of Christ in the same way the priest does, but administer them on the strength of their mandate from the community.'" See Anthony Vanderhaar, *The Relation of the Character of the Priesthood to the Sacramentals* (Rome: Catholic Book Agency, 1965).

23. *Book of Blessings*, nos. 195–214, pp. 96–101.

8. The Nature of Blessings: Disputed Questions

1. Puniet, *The Roman Pontifical: A History and Commentary*, 236.

2. This citation is from New Advent, accessed February 6, 2018, http://www.newadvent.org/summa/4065.htm.

3. Peter Kwasniewski, "St. Thomas on the 'Asperges' (Sprinkling Rite)," published 7 August 2014, http://www.ccwatershed.org/blog/2014/aug/7/st-thomas-asperges-sprinkling-rite/ (accessed 12/29/17).

4. St. Thomas wrote about the relation of holy water and other sacramentals to the sacraments: "Holy Water and other consecrated things are not called sacraments, because they do not produce the sacramental effect, which is the receiving of grace. They are, however, a kind of disposition to the sacraments: either by removing obstacles, thus holy water is ordained

against the snares of the demons, and against venial sins: or by making things suitable for the conferring of a sacrament; thus the altar and vessels are consecrated through reverence for the Eucharist" (*ST* III, q. 65, art. 1, ad 6), taken from New Advent, accessed May 25, 2018, http://www.newadvent.org/summa/4065.htm.

5. Code of Canon Law, no. 1166, accessed February 2, 2018, http://www.vatican.va/archive/ENG1104/_P48.HTM.

6. John L. Paschang, *The Sacramentals according to the Code of Canon Law* (Washington, DC: Kessinger Legacy Reprints, 1925), 32.

7. Henri Leclercq, "Sacramentals," in *The Catholic Encyclopedia*, vol. 13 (New York: Robert Appleton, 1912), as cited at New Advent, accessed May 26, 2018, http://www.newadvent.org/cathen/13292d.htm. See also Paschang, *Sacramentals*, 32–33: "Sacramentals produce their effect not '*ex opera operato*,' but '*ex opera operantis* (*ecclesiae*).' They operate by reason of the supporting prayer of the Church. When the Church makes use of Sacramentals she either '*formaliter*' or '*virtualiter*' asks God to grant a certain effect, and it is in virtue of this prayer of the Church, that the Sacramentals operate. If the effect of the Sacramentals depended principally upon the '*opus operans*' of the subject, then any good work might properly be called a Sacramental, there would be no reason for the distinction between a good work, a pious act and a Sacramental."

8. Paschang, *Sacramentals*, 34.

9. The Roman Ritual, vol. 3, *The Blessings*, trans. and ed. Philip T. Weller (Milwaukee: Bruce Publishing, 1946), 329.

10. Weller, The Roman Ritual, vol. 3, *The Blessings*, 331.

11. Weller, The Roman Ritual, vol. 3, *The Blessings*, 335.

12. Weller, The Roman Ritual, vol. 3, *The Blessings*, 337.

13. "Apotropaic Magic," Wikipedia, accessed December 16, 2017, https://en.wikipedia.org/wiki/Apotropaic_magic; also "Evil Eye," Wikipedia, accessed December 16, 2017, https://en.wikipedia.org/wiki/Evil_eye.

14. "Rabbit's Foot," Wikipedia, accessed December 16, 2017, https://en.wikipedia.org/wiki/Rabbit%27s_foot.

15. The Roman Ritual, *Book of Blessings,* Approved for Use in the Dioceses of the United States of America by the National Conference of Catholic Bishops and Confirmed by the Apostolic See (New York: Catholic Book Publishing, 1989), no. 1455, p. 622.

16. *Book of Blessings,* no. 1479, p. 631.

17. *Book of Blessings,* no. 1487, p. 634.

18. Edward Yarnold, *The Awe-Inspiring Rites of Initiation*, 2nd ed. (Collegeville, MN: Liturgical Press, 1994), 22–23.

19. As quoted in Yarnold, *Awe-Inspiring Rites of Initiation*, 105.

20. As quoted in E. C. Whitaker, *Documents of the Baptismal Liturgy*, revised by Maxwell E. Johnson (Collegeville, MN: Liturgical Press, 2003), 9.

21. As quoted in Yarnold, *Awe-Inspiring Rites of Initiation*, 185. The author's footnote to this citation says, "Note the implication that the water is changed."

22. Former Benedictine monk and then priest of the Archdiocese of Westminster Fr. Henri Leclercq stated, "One of the most remarkable effects of sacramentals is the virtue to drive away evil spirits whose mysterious and baleful operations affect sometimes the physical activity of man." Leclercq, "Sacramentals."

23. The Roman Ritual, *Exorcisms and Related Supplications*, English Translation according to the Typical Edition, for Use in the Dioceses of the United States of America, Approved by the USCCB and Confirmed by the Holy See (Washington, DC: USCCB, 2017), no. 58, p. 27.

24. *Exorcisms and Related Supplications*, no. 21, p. 7.

25. *Exorcisms and Related Supplications*, no. 44, p. 14.

26. *Exorcisms and Related Supplications*, no. 59, p. 28. See also R. Cabié, "Christian Initiation," in *The Sacraments*, vol. 3 of *The Church at Prayer: An Introduction to the Liturgy*, ed. A. G. Martimort et al. (Collegeville, MN: Liturgical Press, 1988), p. 23 and n. 30: "The exsufflation, which calls to mind the breath of God at work in the creation of man, came to be interpreted as exorcistic, a gesture of contempt for the powers of evil operative in creatures."

27. Solemn exorcisms can be performed on persons not baptized with the permission of the local ordinary (see Code of Canon Law, no. 1170). In such a case, the words of the Rite of Exorcism need to be adapted to suit the circumstances.

28. *Exorcisms and Related Supplications*, no. 19, p. 33.

29. Reiner Kaczynski, "Blessings in Rome and the Non-Roman West," in *Sacraments and Sacramentals: Handbook for Liturgical Studies*, vol. 4, ed. Anscar J. Chupungco (Collegeville, MN: Liturgical Press, 2000), 400–401.

30. James Monti, *A Sense of the Sacred: Roman Catholic Worship in the Middle Ages* (San Francisco: Ignatius Press, 2012), 95.

31. Whitaker, *Documents of the Baptismal Liturgy*, 43.

32. In the instruction for the Syriac fifth-century *Testament of Our Lord*, it appears that some of those brought to Baptism were thought to be possessed by demons. The instruction for the bishop's prayer of exorcism reads: "If anyone be in the endurance of anything, rise suddenly while the bishop is saying [these words], and weep or cry out, or foam [at the mouth] or gnash with his teeth, or stare . . . or altogether run away . . . let such an one be exorcized by the priests until he be cleansed, and so let him be baptized. After the priest exorciseth those who have drawn near, or him who is found unclean, let the priest breathe on them and seal them between their eyes, on the nose, on the heart, on the ears; and so let him raise them up." https://archive.org/stream/cu31924029296170/cu31924029296170_djvu.txt, accessed May 26, 2018. See also Yarnold, *Awe-Inspiring Rites of Initiation*, 5: "In the early church pagans were thought to be possessed by the devil." Also Yarnold, *Awe-Inspiring Rites of Initiation*, 11–12: "Zeno of Verona lists some of the reactions which candidates could show to exorcism, such as turning pale, gnashing the teeth, foaming at the mouth, shaking, weeping; presumably the bishop scrutinized the candidate to ascertain that none of these phenomena were present, as they would indicate continuing diabolic influence."

33. Stewart-Sykes, *On the Apostolic Tradition*, 106.

34. Yarnold, *Awe-Inspiring Rites of Initiation*, 6.

35. Stewart-Sykes, *On the Apostolic Tradition*, 109.

36. Henry A. Kelly, *The Devil at Baptism: Ritual, Theology, and Drama* (Eugene, OR: Wipf and Stock, 1985), 113, 150–51. In Yarnold, *Awe-Inspiring Rites of Initiation*, 11: "St. Augustine, while expecting the elect to scrutinize their own hearts, saw the exorcisms as a means of testing whether they were free from the influence of unclean spirits."

37. Kelly, *Devil at Baptism*, 112–13, 275. Also, St. Thomas Aquinas believed that the exorcism prayers were an important part of the baptismal process. He said, "The devil's power to impede the effect of the sacrament is held in check through the prayers, blessings and the like" (*ST* III, q. 66, a. 10) in http://www.newadvent.org/summa/4066.htm#article10, accessed May 26, 2018. While the sacrament is validly conferred in Baptism, "through the rites of exorcism a twofold impediment to the reception of saving grace is removed." St. Thomas cited St. Augustine: "Augustine says, 'Children are breathed on and exorcized in order that the devil's hostile power which deceived man be chased far from them'" (*ST* III, q. 71, a. 3). So according to St. Thomas, the exorcism prayers assisted the

individuals in living out their baptismal grace. In http://www.newadvent.org/summa/4071.htm, accessed May 26, 2018.

38. Whitaker, *Documents of the Baptismal Liturgy*, 12.

39. Whitaker, *Documents of the Baptismal Liturgy*, 270.

40. Whitaker, *Documents of the Baptismal Liturgy*, 121.

41. Monti, *A Sense of the Sacred*, 99.

42. Monti, *A Sense of the Sacred*, 97–101.

43. Monti, *A Sense of the Sacred*, 95.

44. Weller, The Roman Ritual, vol. 3, *The Blessings*, 81.

45. Whitaker, *Documents of the Baptismal Liturgy*, 32. See also Cabié, "Christian Initiation," 39: "This unguent was truly that with which fighters rubbed themselves so that they might be more nimble in the competitions."

46. Yarnold, *Awe-Inspiring Rites of Initiation*, 23.

47. See Nick Squires, "Don't Argue with the Devil, He's Much More Intelligent Than Us, Says Pope Francis," *The Telegraph,* December 13, 2017, http://www.telegraph.co.uk/news/2017/12/13/dont-argue-devil-much-intelligent-us-says-pope-francis/. Pope Francis is quoted as saying, "He is evil. . . . He's not a diffuse thing, he is a person." He applauded the works of exorcists and said they should show "the love and welcome of the Church for those possessed by evil."

48. *Exorcisms and Related Supplications*, no. 1, p. 65.

49. *The Roman Missal*, Appendix II: "Rite for the Blessing and Sprinkling of Water," 1297–98.

50. There has been some question as to whether *Summorum Pontificum* applies to the *Book of Blessings*, although it clearly applies to sacraments. On April 30, 2011, the Pontifical Commission *Ecclesia Dei* issued *Universae Ecclesiae*, which answered the question definitely in the affirmative. Here is the relevant citation: "The use of the *Pontificale Romanum*, the *Rituale Romanum*, as well as the *Caeremoniale Episcoporum* in effect in 1962, is permitted" (no. 35). Found at http://www.vatican.va/roman_curia/pontifical_commissions/ecclsdei/documents/rc_com_ecclsdei_doc_20110430_istr-universae-ecclesiae_en.html, accessed May 26, 2018.

51. "The Scrutinies," no. 141, found at Creighton Online Ministries, accessed December 17, 2017, http://onlineministries.creighton.edu/CollaborativeMinistry/Lent/scrutiny-1.html.

52. Dominic E. Serra, "The Scrutinies: Exorcisms That Make Lent a Joyful Season," *Catechumenate: A Journal of Christian Initiation*, 32, no. 2

(March 2010): 19, 25. See also Yarnold, *Awe-Inspiring Rites of Initiation*, 22, regarding the RCIA anointings: "The first anointing is best understood as a sign of the candidates' release from the power of the devil in preparation for baptism, and their strengthening for the conflict that lies ahead."

53. Augustine, *Lectures or Tractates on the Gospel of St. John*, vol. 2, in *The Works of Aurelius Augustine*, ed. Marcus Dods, trans. James Innes (Edinburgh: T and T Clark, 1884), 300. Found at Google Books, accessed May 25, 2018, https://books.google.com/books?id=AcM4AQAAMAAJ&pg=PA300&lpg=PA300&dq=augustine+Take+away+the+words+and+what+is+the+water+but+just+water&source=bl&ots=71C6QJC9p5&sig=y-99M-NzWthONiybyMkT5zy9Y2j4&hl=en&sa=X&ved=0ahUKEwip3O6zze-jVAhUl4YMKHcyLD3wQ6AEINjAE#v=onepage&q=augustine%20Take%20away%20the%20words%20and%20what%20is%20the%20water%20but%20just%20water&f=false.

54. Uwe Michael Lang, "Theologies of Blessing: Origins and Characteristics of *De benedictionibus* (1984)," *Antiphon* 15, no. 1 (2011): 40.

55. Derek A. Rivard, *Blessing the World: Ritual and Lay Piety in Medieval Religion* (Washington, DC: CUA Press, 2009), 77–78.

56. *Book of Blessings*, nos. 16–17, 20–24, 27, pp. 25, 27–29.

57. *Book of Blessings*, no. 17, p. 25. This interpretation of no. 17 of the *Book of Blessings* is also found in Ryan T. Ruiz, *Inclinate Vos Ad Benedictionem: A Study of the Theological, Pastoral and Cultural Implications of Aptatio/Inculturatio in the Church's Post-Conciliar Rites of Blessing* (Rome: Pontificium Athenaeum S. Anselmi De Urbe, 2016), 300–301.

Summary

1. Derek A. Rivard, *Blessing the World: Ritual and Lay Piety in Medieval Religion* (Washington, DC: CUA Press, 2009), 292.

2. The Roman Ritual, *Book of Blessings,* Approved for Use in the Dioceses of the United States of America by the National Conference of Catholic Bishops and Confirmed by the Apostolic See (New York: Catholic Book Publishing, 1989), no. 19, p. 27.

3. *Book of Blessings*, no. 12, p. 24.

4. *Summorum Pontificum* allows the use of blessings in the Extraordinary Form (EF) that were approved and in effect in 1962 when the Second Vatican Council opened. Fr. Ruiz indicated that the last approved *Collectio* of blessings in the United States at that time was the 1961 *Collectio*, usually

published under the title *Practical Handbook of Rites, Blessings and Prayers* (St. Paul, MN: North Central Publishing, 1961), which includes Latin and some English prayers. The Weller version, cited in this book, is used here as a common resource utilized by priests; however, Fr. Ruiz opines that it is not strictly authorized for usage in blessings under *Summorum Pontificum*. For a source that attempts to provide some authorized English-language blessings in the EF, see Fr. Dylan Schrader's collection of blessings at Ipsissima Verba, accessed February 4, 2018, http://resources.ipsissima-verba.org/documents/extraordinary form-benedictionale-usa-draft-4.pdf. Nevertheless, this work does not have a clear authorization for use by relevant ecclesiastical authority. For a fuller discussion of what translations are authorized, see Ryan T. Ruiz, "Which Version of the *Rituale Romanum* Is Allowed by *Summorum Pontificum*, and Does It Allow Any English Texts?" *Adoremus Bulletin* 22, no. 7 (July 4, 2017).

5. *The Roman Missal*, Appendix II: "Rite for the Blessing and Sprinkling of Water," 1296–98.

6. Keith Edward Kenney, "A Theology of Blessings," Spring 2014, unpublished, p. 40. Cited with permission.

7. Joseph Ratzinger, *The Spirit of the Liturgy*, trans. John Saward (San Francisco: Ignatius Press, 2000), 184.

8. People are especially desirous to have a priest bless them if he has a reputation for holiness. For example, Padre Pio, a now-canonized Italian Capuchin monk and mystic, was deluged in his later life with requests for prayers and blessings by great crowds of people as his reputation for sanctity spread.

SELECTED BIBLIOGRAPHY

Apostolic Constitutions, Book VII, Concerning Deportment, and the Eucharist, and Initiation into Christ, XLIII, "A Thanksgiving concerning the Mystical Water." Accessed December 16, 2017. https://ldsfocuschrist2.files.wordpress.com/2012/03/apostolic-constitutions-william-whiston.pdf.

Benedict XVI. *Omnium in Mentem.* October 26, 2009. http://w2.vatican.va/content/benedict-xvi/en/apost_letters/documents/hf_ben-xvi_apl_20091026_codex-iuris-canonici.html.

Cabié, R. "Christian Initiation." In *The Sacraments,* vol. 3 of *The Church at Prayer: An Introduction to the Liturgy,* edited by A. G. Martimort et al., 11–100. Collegeville, MN: Liturgical Press, 1988.

Collins, Mary, and David Power, eds. *Concilium: Blessing and Power* 178, no. 2 (1985).

Hauke, Manfred. "The Theological Battle over the Rite of Exorcism, 'Cinderella' of the New *Rituale Romanum.*" *Antiphon* 10, no. 1 (2006): 32–69.

Irwin, Kevin. "A Sacramental World: Sacramentality as the Primary Language for Sacraments." *Worship* 76, no. 3 (May 2002): 197–211.

Jounel, P. "Blessings." In *The Sacraments,* vol. 3 of *The Church at Prayer: An Introduction to the Liturgy,* edited by A. G. Martimort et al., 263–84. Collegeville, MN: Liturgical Press, 1988.

Kaczynski, Reiner. "Blessings in Rome and the Non-Roman West." In *Sacraments and Sacramentals: Handbook for Liturgical Studies,* vol. 4, edited by Anscar J. Chupungco, 393–410. Collegeville, MN: Liturgical Press, 2000.

Kenney, Keith Edward. "A Theology of Blessings." Spring 2014, unpublished.

LaChance, Steven A. *Confrontation with Evil: An In-Depth Review of the 1949 Possession That Inspired "The Exorcist."* Woodbury, MN: Llewellyn Publications, 2017.

Lang, Uwe Michael. "Theologies of Blessing: Origins and Characteristics of *De benedictionibus* (1984)." *Antiphon* 15, no. 1 (2011): 27–46.

Macmurrough, Carol. "The Blessing of Homes: Roman Rite." *Orate Fratres* 14, no. 5 (March 17, 1940): 201–3.

McKenzie, John L. "Curse." In *Dictionary of the Bible*, 165–66. New York: Macmillan, 1965.

Monti, James. *A Sense of the Sacred: Roman Catholic Worship in the Middle Ages*. San Francisco: Ignatius Press, 2012.

Paschang, John L. *The Sacramentals according to the Code of Canon Law*. Washington, DC: Kessinger Legacy Reprints, 1925.

Puniet, Dom Pierre de, O.S.B. *The Roman Pontifical: A History and Commentary*. New York: Longmans, Green, 1932.

Ratzinger, Joseph. *The Spirit of the Liturgy*. Translated by John Saward. San Francisco: Ignatius Press, 2000.

Rivard, Derek A. *Blessing the World: Ritual and Lay Piety in Medieval Religion*. Washington, DC: CUA Press, 2009.

The Roman Missal. Appendix II: "Rite for the Blessing and Sprinkling of Water," 1296–99. English Translation according to the Third Typical Edition, for Use in the Dioceses of the United States of America, Approved by the USCCB and Confirmed by the Apostolic See. Totowa, NJ: Catholic Book Publishing, 2011.

The Roman Ritual. *Book of Blessings*. Approved for Use in the Dioceses of the United States of America by the National Conference of Catholic Bishops and Confirmed by the Apostolic See. New York: Catholic Book Publishing, 1989.

———. *Exorcisms and Related Supplications*. English Translation according to the Typical Edition, for Use in the Dioceses of the United States of America, Approved by the USCCB and Confirmed by the Holy See. Washington, DC: USCCB, 2017.

———. Vol. 3, *The Blessings*. Translated and edited by Philip T. Weller. Milwaukee: Bruce Publishing, 1946.

Ruiz, Ryan T. *Inclinate Vos Ad Benedictionem: A Study of the Theological, Pastoral and Cultural Implications of Aptatio/Inculturatio in the Church's Post-Conciliar Rites of Blessing*. Rome: Pontificium Athenaeum S. Anselmi De Urbe, 2016.

Scharbert, Josef. "Blessing." In *Encyclopedia of Biblical Theology: The Complete Sacramentum Verbi*, edited by J. B. Bauer, 69–74. New York: Crossroad, 1981.

Second Vatican Council. Constitution on the Sacred Liturgy, *Sacrosanctum Concilium*. December 4, 1963. http://www.vatican.va/archive/hist_councils/ii_vatican_council/documents/vat-ii_const_19631204_sacrosanctum-concilium_en.html.

Serra, Dominic E. "The Blessing of Baptismal Water at the Paschal Vigil: Ancient Texts and Modern Revisions." *Worship* 64 (1990): 142–56.

———. "The Scrutinies: Exorcisms That Make Lent a Joyful Season." *Catechumenate: A Journal of Christian Initiation* 32, no. 2 (March 2010): 19–27.

Stewart-Sykes, Alistair. *On the Apostolic Tradition*. An English Version with Introduction and Commentary. Crestwood, NY: St. Vladimir's Seminary Press, 2001.

Theiler, Henry. *Holy Water and Its Significance for Catholics*. Translated by Rev. J. F. Lang. New York: Fr. Pustet, 1909.

Van Slyke, Daniel G. "The Order for Blessing Water: Past and Present." *Antiphon* 8, no. 2 (2003): 12–23.

———. "Toward a Theology of Blessings: Agents and Recipients of Benedictions." *Antiphon* 15, no. 1 (2011): 47–60.

Westermann, Claus. *Blessing in the Bible and Life of the Church*. Translated by Keith Crim. Philadelphia: Fortress Press, 1978.

Whitaker, E. C. *Documents of the Baptismal Liturgy*. Revised by Maxwell E. Johnson. Collegeville, MN: Liturgical Press, 2003.

Wilson, H. A., ed. *The Gelasian Sacramentary: Liber Sacramentorum Romanae Ecclesiae*. Oxford: Clarendon Press, 1894. Found at US Archive. Accessed January 20, 2018. https://ia902701.us.archive.org/7/items/gelasiansacrame00gelagoog/gelasiansacrame00gelagoog.pdf.

Yarnold, Edward. *The Awe-Inspiring Rites of Initiation*, 2nd ed. Collegeville, MN: Liturgical Press, 1994.

Msgr. Stephen J. Rossetti, a priest of the Diocese of Syracuse, is an expert on priestly spirituality and wellness issues. He is a Catholic speaker, educator, psychologist, and retreat leader. He served for many years at Saint Luke Institute in Maryland, rising to president and CEO. A graduate of the United States Air Force Academy, Rossetti earned a doctorate in psychology from Boston College and a doctor of ministry from the Catholic University of America. Rossetti is the author or editor of ten books, including *Born of the Eucharist*, *Letters to My Brothers*, and *The Joy of Priesthood*—the recipient of a Catholic Press Association book award. He serves as research associate professor of pastoral studies at the Catholic University and a visiting professor at Gregorian University in Rome.

Rossetti received a Proclaim Award from the United States Conference of Catholic Bishops as well as a Lifetime Service Award from the Theological College of the Catholic University of America. In 2010, he received the Touchstone Award from the National Federation of Priests' Councils for a lifetime of work with priests. In 2013, Rossetti received the Pope John Paul II Seminary Leadership Award from National Catholic Educational Association for distinguished service in priestly formation and was awarded a doctor of divinity degree, honoris causa, from St. Mary's Seminary and University.